New Era, New Asian Games, New Canal

China Stories about the Grand Canal

Zhang Youguo, Chief Editor

新时代 新亚运 新运河

运河中国

张友国 主编

中国摄影出版传媒有限责任公司
China Photographic Publishing & Media Co.,Ltd.
中国摄影出版社

"运河中国"首届影像

热烈欢迎大运河沿线摄影家莅临临平采风

艺术周暨影像大展合影

2023.6 杭州·临平

目录
CONTENTS

封面、封底摄影：李盛韬

序一

　　2023年6月，我有幸见证了"运河中国"首届影像艺术周暨影像大展在杭州临平隆重开幕，运河文化领域与摄影界的专家学者齐聚大运河古镇塘栖，就"运河的影像叙事"进行学术研讨。这不仅仅是一场影像艺术活动，更是对中国大运河千年历史的影像致敬，是一次文化传承与创新的交响，意义非凡。

　　运河，是人类适应生存发展的需求，依靠当时的技术能力，结合自然条件而兴建的水利工程。运河文化源远流长，运河精神生生不息，运河工程前后相继。中国的运河文化在世界上独树一帜，根深叶茂，传承千载，历久弥新，是一脉活态的历史文化传承，时代的流变对运河的影响巨大。运河与长城并列，成为中华民族人文精神的伟大象征。

　　摄影诞生并传入中国后，运河开始有了影像记录，如今它们成为珍贵的影像文献，对运河文化的研究有着不可替代的价值和作用。中国的运河文化是世界运河文化的重要组成部分。中国的运河记录是中国故事的影像声音，必将为"一带一路"和人类命运共同体建设做出积极的贡献。

　　今天的影像就是明天的历史。但摄影艺术的作用又不仅仅体现在历史价值上，它还是时代的火炬和号角，具有无与伦比的传播力，能够直接促进经济、社会、文化的发展，是不可忽视的生产力。

　　作为一名摄影人，我深切地感受着影像力量在运河文化中的绽放。它超越语言，直抵人心，将大运河的壮美与沧桑、人民的智慧与勤劳凝固于永恒的瞬间。这次影像展汇聚了众多摄影家和艺术家的心血，他们用镜头捕捉了运河沿岸的多元文化与风土人情，记录了时代变迁与发展轨迹，为我们呈现了一幅波澜壮阔的历史画卷。

　　杭州，这座浸润千年运河记忆的城市，为这次展览提供了完美的舞台。展览的成功举办，离不开杭州作为"大运河摄影发展联盟"发起地的深厚积淀，离不开"大运河摄影发展联盟"发起人及其同仁的辛勤付出。

　　大运河摄影发展联盟，是新时代中国摄影人钟情于运河文化的一个有理想、有作为的组织。自2019年联盟成立以来，我一直关注并参与着联盟的各项活动。在短短5年的时间里，联盟大胆探索，奋发有为，从无到有，从弱到强，由浅入深，一步一个脚印，为大运河影像的传播搭建了平台，也为沿线城市的文化旅游和经济发展注入了新的活力，不断取得社会的认可、政府的支持和摄影界的赞誉，对大运河影像文化建设做出了突出的贡献，确实可敬可贺！

　　《运河中国》的出版，则是对本次展览的延续和升华。它将展览的精华凝结成册，使其得以永久保存和传播。这本画册既是一份艺术珍品，更是一部珍贵的历史文献。它将大运河的故事传递给更多的人，让更多的人了解和关注这条流淌千年的文化长河。

　　浙江作为中国大运河文化的集大成者，拥有运河影像文化建设的生力军，更有钟情于运河文化、支持影像发展的政府和民间力量，他们对运河文化建设的作为和贡献令人钦佩。

　　运河的影像文化是一个宏大多元的摄影主题，需要我们以先进的理念、宽阔的视野，进行大胆而深入的摄影实践、恢宏而缜密的学术研究。我相信，在大家的共同努力下，大运河影像文化的品牌将更加璀璨夺目，闪烁出新时代的光彩，成为中国影像大厦的支柱。

中国摄影家协会副主席
大运河摄影发展联盟顾问　　杨越峦

Preface 1

In June 2023, I had the honor of witnessing the grand opening of "China Stories about the Grand Canal" Image Art Week and Exhibition in Linping, Hangzhou. Experts and scholars from the field of canal culture and photography gathered in Tangqi, a historic town along the Grand Canal, to hold academic discussions on "Narratives of the Grand Canal in Images." This event was not merely an artistic endeavor but also a tribute to the thousand-year history of the Grand Canal in China, signifying a symphony of cultural inheritance and innovation, with profound significance.

The Grand Canal, born out of the human need for survival and development, was constructed as a water conservancy project combining technological capabilities of the time with natural conditions. With a long and enduring history, the spirit of the Grand Canal persists, witnessing the successive stages of its construction. Chinese canal culture stands out uniquely in the world, deeply rooted and flourishing, embodying a dynamic heritage of history and culture. The changes of the times have had a profound impact on the Grand Canal, making it alongside the Great Wall, a great symbol of the cultural spirit of the Chinese nation.

Since the advent of photography in China, documenting the Grand Canal through imagery has become a valuable documentary resource, contributing irreplaceable value to the study of canal culture. Chinese canal culture is an integral part of the world's canal culture. The photographic records of the Grand Canal in China serve as visual narratives of Chinese stories, making significant contributions to the construction of the Belt and Road Initiative and a community with a shared future for mankind.

Today's images are tomorrow's history, yet the role of photographic art extends beyond its historical value. It serves as a torch and a clarion call of the times, possessing unparalleled communicative power, directly promoting economic, social, and cultural development, constituting an indispensable productive force.

As a photographer, I deeply appreciate the power of images in canal culture. Transcending language, they reach the heart, capturing the grandeur and vicissitudes of the Grand Canal, the wisdom and diligence of the people, freezing them in eternal moments. This image exhibition has brought together the efforts of numerous photographers and artists, capturing the diverse cultures and local customs along the Grand Canal, documenting the trajectory of development and change over time, presenting a magnificent historical panorama.

Hangzhou, a city steeped in the memories of the Grand Canal for millennia, provided a perfect stage for this exhibition. The successful hosting of the exhibition owes much to the deep accumulation of Hangzhou as the birthplace of the "Grand Canal Photography Development Alliance" and the diligent efforts of its founders and colleagues.

The Grand Canal Photography Development Alliance represents a new organization of Chinese photographers in the new era. Since its establishment in 2019, I have been following and participating in various activities of the alliance. In just five years, the alliance has boldly explored, worked hard, progressed from nothing to something, from weakness to strength, gradually delving deeper, step by step, establishing a platform for the dissemination of Grand Canal imagery, injecting new vitality into the cultural tourism and economic development of cities along the route, continually gaining social recognition, government support, and acclaim from the photography community, making outstanding contributions to the construction of Grand Canal image culture, truly commendable!

China Stories about the Grand Canal is a continuation and elevation of this exhibition. It condenses the essence of the exhibition into a book, ensuring its permanent preservation and dissemination. This album is not only an artistic treasure but also a valuable historical document, transmitting the story of the Grand Canal to more people, allowing more people to understand and pay attention to this cultural river that has flowed for thousands of years.

As a culmination of Chinese Grand Canal culture, Zhejiang Province has become a strong force in the construction of canal image culture, supported by governments and private entities passionate about canal culture and image development, their efforts and contributions to canal culture construction are admirable.

The image culture of the Grand Canal is a vast and diverse photographic theme, requiring us to engage in bold and in-depth photographic practices with advanced concepts and broad perspectives, as well as grand and meticulous academic research. I believe that with everyone's concerted efforts, the brand of Grand Canal image culture will shine even brighter, radiating the brilliance of the new era, becoming the backbone of China's image architecture.

Vice Chairman of China Photographers Association
Consultant of Grand Canal Photography Development Alliance
Yang Yueluan

序二

　　悠悠运河，连通南北，成就了一座座城市的繁荣发展。杭州市临平区处于杭嘉湖平原，大运河文化积淀深厚、资源丰富，京杭大运河（杭州塘）、古运河（上塘河）和临平运河（京杭大运河杭州段运河二通道）等三条运河贯穿而过，河道总长约 56 公里，有世界文化遗产河段 2 个、遗产点 1 个、遗址群 6 个、不可移动文物 100 余处，其中广济桥是大运河上仅存的一座七孔石桥。

　　为深入贯彻习近平总书记关于大运河文化保护传承利用的重要指示精神，临平区积极从运河中汲取发展精神动力，弘扬"兼收并蓄，包容开放""开拓创新，追求卓越""润泽万物，美美与共"的精神，推进优秀传统文化的创造性转化、创新性发展。临平区一方面打造景观运河、致富运河，焕发古运河的新时代风貌；另一方面打造人文运河、魅力运河，引领大运河文化的创新发展。一幅流域环境持续改善、区域经济高质量发展、文化氛围不断浓郁的运河两岸美好画卷正徐徐展开。

　　近年来，临平区按照保护是前提、利用是过程、传承发展是目的原则，全力实施以"古今运河、时尚临平"为核心的新时代文化临平建设工程，积极推进大运河国家文化公园（临平段）、上塘河宋韵文化带建设，通过加强历史文物保护、优化文化遗存展现、增强文化价值阐释、强化文化活态传承、严格生态保护修复等举措，打造 29 公里大运河绿道，建成临平俞樾纪念馆、临平山历史文化陈列馆、安隐寺（安平泉）遗址公园、朱炳仁大运河艺术馆、"临平造"品牌传播中心等大运河沿线文化地标，成立中国大运河古镇联盟，举办大运河古镇发展文化周活动、"运河中国"首届影像艺术周暨影像大展、"行走大运河"全民健身健步走等大运河主题活动，唱好古今运河交响曲。大运河文化（临平段）已入选全省首批"浙江文化标识"培育项目、全省 11 个省级文化传承生态保护区名单。

　　本次"运河中国"首届影像艺术周暨摄影大展旨在围绕"中国新时代·杭州新亚运"主题，以影像艺术形式深入挖掘大运河杭州段及其沿线故事，展示大运河丰厚的历史文化遗产、优美的自然人文景观和幸福美好的人民生活。活动期间，众多专家、学者、媒体人到杭州临平参加大运河影像文化学术研讨会、大运河（临平段）采风创作系列活动，并在杭州临平成立了"运河中国"首届影像艺术驻地创作营。

　　一条运河，贯通南北跨越古今；一湾河水，串联两岸秀丽河山。临平区将持续在大运河保护中优先推动可持续发展，努力打造世界文化遗产保护范例，努力打响塘栖"京杭大运河南源首镇"品牌，弘扬临平大运河文化时代新风。

中共杭州市临平区委常委、宣传部部长　　沈　威

The Grand Canal, linking the north and south, has fostered the prosperity and development of numerous cities. Linping District, situated in the Hangjiahu Plain, boasts a rich cultural heritage and abundant resources related to the Grand Canal. Three canals, namely the Beijing-Hangzhou Grand Canal (Hangzhou Section), the Ancient Canal (Shangtang River), and the Linping Canal (Second Channel of the Beijing-Hangzhou Grand Canal in Hangzhou Section), traverse the area, with a total length of approximately 56 kilometers. This section features two UNESCO World Heritage sites, one heritage point, six site clusters, and over 100 immovable cultural relics, among which the Guangji Bridge stands as the only remaining seven-arch stone bridge on the Grand Canal.

In line with the important instructions from General Secretary Xi Jinping regarding the protection, inheritance, and utilization of Grand Canal culture, Linping District actively draws development inspiration from the canal, promoting the era's spirit of "inclusive openness, innovative pursuit, and shared beauty". It advances the creative transformation and innovative development of excellent traditional culture. On one hand, it revitalizes the ancient canal's new era charm by creating scenic and prosperous canal areas. On the other hand, it leads the innovative development of Grand Canal culture by establishing a cultural canal and fostering its allure. A beautiful picture is gradually unfolding along the canal's banks, depicting continuous improvement of the basin environment, high-quality regional economic development, and a continuously enriched cultural atmosphere.

In recent years, Linping District has vigorously implemented the construction of the "Ancient and Modern Canal, Fashionable Linping" project, with the principle of "protection as the premise, utilization as the process, and inheritance and development as the goal". It actively promotes the construction of the Grand Canal National Cultural Park (Linping Section) and the Shangtang River Song Dynasty Cultural Belt. Through measures such as strengthening the protection of historical relics, optimizing the display of cultural heritage, enhancing cultural value interpretation, strengthening dynamic cultural inheritance, and rigorously protecting and restoring the ecology, it has created a 29-kilometer greenway along the Grand Canal. Cultural landmarks such as the Linping Yu Yue Memorial Hall, Linping Mountain Historical and Cultural Exhibition Hall, Anyin Temple (Anping Spring) Site Park, Zhu Bingren Grand Canal Art Museum, and "Linping Made" Brand Communication Center have been established along the Grand Canal. The China Grand Canal Ancient Town Alliance has been established, and activities such as the Grand Canal Ancient Town Development Theme Event, the "China Stories about the Grand Canal" Image Art Week and Exhibition, and the "Walking the Grand Canal" National Fitness Walking Event have been organized, singing the symphony of the ancient and modern Grand Canal.The Grand Canal culture (Linping Section) has been selected as one of the first batch of "Zhejiang Cultural Symbols" cultivation projects and listed in the province's 11 provincial-level cultural inheritance ecological protection areas.

"China Stories about the Grand Canal" Image Art Week and Exhibition aims to explore the stories along the Hangzhou Section of the Grand Canal and its surroundings in the form of image art, under the theme of "China's New Era, Hangzhou's New Asian Games", showcasing the rich historical and cultural heritage, beautiful natural and cultural landscapes, and the happy and beautiful lives of the people along the Grand Canal. During the event, numerous experts, scholars, and media professionals have been invited to Linping, Hangzhou, to participate in academic seminars on Grand Canal image culture and a series of creative activities on Grand Canal exploration and creation. The "Canal China" First Image Art Residency Creation Camp has also been established in Linping, Hangzhou.

A canal connecting the north and south, traversing ancient and modern times; a river winding through, linking picturesque landscapes on both banks. Linping District will continue to promote sustainable development with Grand Canal protection as a priority, striving to create a model for the protection of world cultural heritage and to establish the brand of "Tangqi, the First Town of the Southern Source of the Beijing-Hangzhou Grand Canal". It will promote the new era of Linping Grand Canal culture.

The Chief of the Publicity Department of Hangzhou Linping District Committee of CPC　　Shen Wei

序三

河流是部文明史（展览前言）

河流对文明进程造成的影响超乎我们的想象。河流是古文明的动脉，人类灿烂的文明遗产几乎都离不开河流的哺育。一方面，河流提供了水资源和交通方式，使早期人类的繁衍与交流成为可能。随着文明的发展进步，河流又推动了农业、工业、贸易进程，提供了新型能源，为社会繁荣提供了动力。另一方面，河流作为一种天然的屏障，也催生了民族文化认同，对人口迁徙、生活方式、社会结构、生态健康等造成了深远影响。

一条大河，跨越 10 多个纬度，绵延近 3200 余公里，流过 2500 多个春秋。地理上的体验与勘察可以为人文学科提供具体且富有启示的发现和思考，构成不同视野的疏通致远。在整个人类历史发展中，我们对河流的着迷经由艺术、文学和图像显露而出。作为中华民族长盛不衰的重要文化载体，京杭大运河一直在图像中流淌，也在摄影艺术家的镜头里蜿蜒穿行。近年来，几代关注运河的影像艺术家，或行走或生活于运河流域，运河成为他们艺术生产中最显而易见的创作场所。他们实地考察、悉心记录，结合当下的问题与思考，激活宏阔历史与城市更新、日常生活的隐微关联。他们顺河而下，体察运河流变、人境迁移，探寻人与天地交融所生发出来的生命力量。

生命如水，岁月如流，运河影像之所以日益受到关注，是因为它们在寻觅历史的同时，并不仅限于从学术上探究问题的答案，而是思索今天人们对历史的认识是如何被建构的。驱动他们行走的思想动力来自对当下的思考和发问。在这个意义上，"运河中国"首届影像艺术周暨影像大展以艺术家在地创作为方法，拓扑河流以及两岸的过去与现在、物理与精神生活，也可为理解当下提供一种路径。艺术家们的创作给我们展现了人与人之间超越地域、风物、文化等建构而相互连通的生存经验、感受。

"运河中国"首届影像艺术周暨影像大展叙事结构主要从两个工作方向展开。一个方向是不断回到中国 20 世纪下半叶的艺术与思想的现场中，认识和梳理国家发展中的历史进程，挖掘在今天仍发挥着影响的文明线索、摄影语言和艺术观念，为中国当代大运河影像研究的学科建设做出持续的努力，这一部分展示的是运河的文明史。另一个同等重要的面向，是专注当下运河沿岸的艺术生产和人文变迁，用议题式的展览来及时把握运河沿岸的文化、社会和城市变革，提出将大运河作为该项目的切入口，试图在展示空间中达到一种文献与作品的共同生长状态，这一部分展示的是运河两岸不同的自然资源和人文资源。

河流是美丽的，但它们对我们的影响远超审美价值。无论如何，河流都是我们赖以生存的根本。这条贯通于隋唐，有着千年历史、千里长度的京杭大运河，在中国版图上，与长城形成了纵横相向的两大人工奇迹，不断延伸着，繁衍着进步和文明，是中华民族的骄傲。运河把海河、黄河、淮河、长江、钱塘江五大水系编连在一起，成为纵贯南北的经济命脉，流淌出说不尽、道不完、看不够的风情、民俗、古迹，积累了丰富的文化底蕴。

让我们一起沿河而下，在京杭大运河的重镇杭州临平相遇。

中国摄影家协会理事

中国摄影家协会策展委员会委员　崔　波

福建省华光摄影艺术博物馆馆长

Preface 2

Rivers : A History of Civilization (Exhibition Preface)

The impact of rivers on the progress of civilization surpasses our imagination. Rivers serve as the arteries of ancient civilizations, and the brilliant heritage of humanity is almost inseparable from the nurturing of rivers. On one hand, rivers provide water resources and transportation, making the reproduction and communication of early humans possible. As civilization developed, rivers further propelled the processes of agriculture, industry, and trade, providing new sources of energy and driving societal prosperity. On the other hand, rivers, as natural barriers, also gave rise to ethnic cultural identity, profoundly influencing population migration, lifestyles, social structures, and ecological health.

A great river, spanning over ten latitudes, stretching nearly 3200 kilometers, passing through over 2500 springs and autumns. Geographical experiences and surveys can provide specific and insightful discoveries and reflections for humanities disciplines, forming channels for different perspectives to connect and extend far. Throughout the course of human history, our fascination with rivers has been revealed through art, literature, and imagery. As an enduring carrier of Chinese culture, the Grand Canal has been flowing in images and winding through the lenses of photographic artists. In recent years, several generations of image artists focusing on the Canal, whether traveling or living in its basin, have made it their most visible creative space. Through on-site investigations and careful documentation, combined with contemporary issues and reflections, they activate the broad historical and urban renewal, as well as the subtle connections of daily life. They follow the river downstream, observe the changes of the Canal and the shifts of human-environment interaction, explore the vitality generated by the integration of humanity and nature.

Life flows like water, time passes like a river. The increasing attention to Canal imagery stems from the fact that, while seeking history, they are not limited to academic exploration of answers, but also ponder how today's understanding of history is constructed. The driving force behind their journey lies in their contemporary thoughts and questions. In this sense, the "China Stories about the Grand Canal" Image Art Week and Exhibition uses artists' on-site creation as a method to map out the past and present of the river and its banks, the physical and spiritual life, also offering a pathway to understanding the present. The artists' creations show us the interconnected experiences and feelings of survival beyond geographical, scenic, and cultural boundaries.

The narrative structure of the "China Stories about the Grand Canal" Image Art Week and Exhibition mainly unfolds in two directions. One direction constantly revisits the scenes of art and thought in the second half of the 20th century China, recognizing and sorting out the historical processes of national development, digging out the civilization clues, photographic language, and artistic concepts that still influence today, and making sustained efforts for the disciplinary construction of contemporary Chinese Grand Canal image research. This part showcases the civilization history of the Canal. Another equally important aspect focuses on the current artistic production and humanistic changes along the Canal, using thematic exhibitions to timely grasp the cultural, social, and urban changes along the Canal. The proposal is to use the Grand Canal as the entry point of this project, attempting to achieve a co-growth state of documents and works in the exhibition space. This part displays the different natural and cultural resources on both sides of the Canal.

Rivers are beautiful, but their impact on us far exceeds aesthetic value. Nonetheless, rivers are the fundamental basis of our existence. The Grand Canal, which has a thousand-year history and spans thousands of miles, has formed a longitudinal and horizontal marvel on the map of China alongside the Great Wall since the Sui and Tang dynasties. It continues to extend, propagate progress and civilization, and is the pride of the Chinese nation. Connecting the Haihe River, Yellow River, Huaihe River, Yangtze River, and Qiantang River, the five major water systems, the Canal serves as the economic lifeline running through the north and south, flowing with an inexhaustible charm, folklore, and historical sites, accumulating rich cultural heritage.

Let us journey down the river together and meet in Linping, the strategic town of the Grand Canal in Hangzhou.

Council Member of the China Photographers Association
Member of the Curatorial Committee of the China Photographers Association   Cui Bo
Director of the Fujian Huaguang Photography Art Museum

溯源寻影：中国大运河最早影像

Tracing the Roots: Earliest Images of the Grand Canal

位于杭州塘栖附近的军营堡。1859 年，丹尼斯·路易·李阁郎（法国）
Fortified military camp near Tangqi, Hangzhou. 1859, photographed by Dennis Louis Legrand (France)

嘉兴茶禅寺三塔。1859 年，丹尼斯·路易·李阁郎（法国）
Three Pagodas of the Tea Zen Temple in Jiaxing.1859, photographed by Dennis Louis Legrand (France)

蛋白立体照片 张友国提供
3D Protein Photograph,Provided by Zhang Youguo

苏州虎丘。1859 年，丹尼斯·路易·李阁郎（法国）
Tiger Hill, Suzhou.1859, photographed by Dennis Louis Legrand (France)

苏州河道上的船只。1859 年，丹尼斯·路易·李阁郎（法国）
Boats on the Suzhou River.1859, photographed by Dennis Louis Legrand (France)

水韵流年：私人珍藏运河老照片

Private Collection: Vintage Photos of the Grand Canal

流淌着的影像之河

早期的大运河影像大多出自国外摄影师。

1859 年，法国人丹尼斯·路易·李阁郎乘船从上海到杭州，经过临平塘栖古镇时，拍摄了一张塘栖运河岸上军营堡的照片，这是目前已知最早的大运河影像之一。

李阁郎同时期还沿大运河去了嘉兴、苏州、宁波等地，沿途拍摄了一些大运河照片。

中国大运河的影像体系由此开始建立。

1864 年太平天国运动结束以后，中国进入休养生息期，越来越多的外国摄影师来华，形成了影像记录中国的第一个热潮。虽然大运河的影像夹杂在其他影像之中，但我们还是可以从中看到彼时大运河的风貌。

1900 年，"庚子国变"爆发，八国联军攻进北京，一批随军摄影师得以进入中国北方，后来又有一些外国摄影师闻讯而来。这些外国摄影师拍摄八国联军军事行动，对重要运输通道的北运河从空中到地面都进行了拍摄，留下了大量北运河影像。后来，其中一些摄影师从北京沿大运河南下，和其他外国摄影师一道，拍摄运河沿线重要城镇，有的甚至再沿浙东运河到宁波，他们的拍摄带来了大运河影像的丰富期。

20 世纪 20 年代至 30 年代初，中国社会由分裂、动荡逐渐走向相对稳定，国内工商业迅猛发展。这时，中国本土照相馆和摄影师已经走向成熟，成为中国摄影的主要力量。特别是五四运动以后，一批经过新文化运动洗礼的文人，如郎静山、吴中行、金石声、黄笃初也加入摄影行列，创作了一系列个性明显、艺术性强的摄影作品，这其中也有不少大运河作品。

这个时期，国内内河运输业、旅游业迅猛发展，来华经商旅游的外国人越来越多。一些外国游客和摄影师常常从上海出发，沿着大运河到杭州、苏州或镇江，再沿长江逆流而上过三峡到四川，边旅游边拍摄，记录旅游过程和沿岸风景人文。这是江南运河影像的又一个丰富期。

20 世纪 30-40 年代，虽然经历抗日战争和解放战争，但仍有不少国内外摄影师用镜头对准大运河。

1949 年后，伴随着运河的生态修复与整治改造，以及运河文化的挖掘表现，大运河影像变得多姿多彩。一代又一代摄影记者、摄影师用影像记录着大运河的变迁与荣光、文化与传承。

斗转星移，沧海桑田。虽然大运河几经变迁，但拍摄大运河的快门声不曾停止过。

大运河是运输之河、人文之河，也是影像之河。

浙江省摄影家协会副主席
杭州市摄影家协会主席　　张友国
大运河摄影发展联盟发起人
大运河老照片收藏者

The Flowing River of Images

Early images of the Grand Canal mostly originated from foreign photographers. In 1859, Frenchman Dennis Louis Legrand traveled by boat from Shanghai to Hangzhou. Passing through the ancient town of Linping Tangqi, he captured a photograph of the military camp fortress on the canal bank, one of the earliest known images of the Grand Canal to date. During the same period, Legrand also traveled to Jiaxing, Suzhou, Ningbo, and other places along the Grand Canal, capturing some photographs along the way. Thus began the establishment of the visual documentation system of the Grand Canal in China.

After the end of the Taiping Rebellion in 1864, China entered a period of recuperation, during which an increasing number of foreign photographers arrived in the country, marking the onset of the first wave of image recording in China. Although images of the Grand Canal were mixed with others, they still provide glimpses of the appearance of the Grand Canal during that time.

In 1900, the "Gengzi Incident" (Boxer Rebellion) erupted, and the Eight-Nation Alliance forces invaded Beijing. A group of military photographers accompanying the troops gained access to northern China, followed by other foreign photographers who arrived upon hearing the news. These foreign photographers documented the military operations of the Eight-Nation Alliance and captured extensive images of the North Canal, an important transportation route, from both aerial and ground perspectives, leaving behind a wealth of visual records of the canal. Later, some of these photographers traveled south along the Grand Canal from Beijing, joining other foreign photographers to document important towns along the canal. Some even continued along the Zhedong Canal to Ningbo. Their work marked a flourishing period of imagery related to the Grand Canal.

In the 1920s and early 1930s, as Chinese society gradually transitioned from fragmentation and turmoil to relative stability, the domestic industry and commerce developed rapidly. During this period, Chinese local photo studios and photographers matured, becoming the main force in Chinese photography. Especially after the May Fourth Movement, a group of literati, such as Lang Jingshan, Wu Zhongxing, Jin Shisheng, and Huang Duchu, who were influenced by the New Culture Movement, also joined the ranks of photographers, creating a series of distinctive and artistic photographic works, including many related to the Grand Canal.

During this period, the domestic river transportation and tourism industries flourished, attracting an increasing number of foreign businessmen and tourists to China. Some foreign visitors and photographers often embarked from Shanghai, following the Grand Canal to Hangzhou, Suzhou, or Zhenjiang, then upstream along the Yangtze River to the Three Gorges and Sichuan, documenting the journey and the scenery and culture along the riverbanks.This period marked another period of richness in images of the Grand Canal in Jiangnan.

In the 1930s and 1940s, despite the anti-Japanese War and the War of Liberation, many domestic and foreign photographers continued to focus their lenses on the Grand Canal.

After 1949, with the restoration and renovation of the Grand Canal and the excavation and expression of its cultural heritage, images of the Grand Canal became colorful. Generation after generation of photojournalists and photographers used images to record the changes and glory, culture, and inheritance of the Grand Canal.

Time passes, and the world changes. Though the Grand Canal has undergone many changes, the sound of shutters capturing its image has never ceased.

The Grand Canal is a river of transportation, a river of culture, and also a river of images.

Vice Chairman of the Zhejiang Provincial Photographers Association
Chairman of the Hangzhou Photographers Association
Founder of the Grand Canal Photography Development Alliance
Collector of old photos of the Grand Canal

Zhang Youguo

对页上：**苏州城墙外大运河。**19 世纪 80 年代，佚名摄，蛋白照片，韩一飞收藏
对页下：**嘉兴茶禅寺三塔。**20 世纪 10 年代，佚名摄，蛋白照片，江建平收藏
　　上：**停泊在北京运河上的漕运粮船。**20 世纪初，佚名摄，火棉胶照片，徐忠民收藏
　　下：**宁波运河上的单孔石拱桥。**19 世纪 70 年代，佚名摄，蛋白纸基，徐忠民收藏

Opposite Above: **Grand Canal outside the Walls of Suzhou.** 1880s, Photographer Unknown, Albumen Print, Collected by Han Yifei
Opposite Below: **Three Pagodas of Tea Zen Temple in Jiaxing.** 1910s, Photographer Unknown, Albumen Print, Collected by Jiang Jianping
Above: **Grain Ships of the Grand Canal Moored in Beijing.** Early 1900s, Photographer Unknown, Collodion Print, Collected by Xu Zhongmin
Below: **Single-Arch Stone Bridge on the Ningbo Canal.** 1870s, Photographer Unknown, Albumen Paper Base, Collected by Xu Zhongmin

对页上：**桐乡双桥**。19 世纪 80 年代，佚名摄，蛋白照片，江建平收藏
对页下：**运河船只"翻坝"景观**。20 世纪 10 年代，佚名摄，火棉胶照片，董桂萍收藏
　　上：**运河上的火轮船**。20 世纪 10 年代，佚名摄，银盐照片（手工着淡彩），楼立伟收藏

Opposite Above: **Tongxiang Double Bridges** . 1880s, Photographer Unknown, Albumen Print, Collection of Jiang Jianping
Opposite Below: **Grand Canal Boat "Turning the Barrier" Scene** . 1910s, Photographer Unknown, Collodion Print, Collection of Dong Guiping
Above: **Steamboat on the Grand Canal** . 1910s, Photographer Unknown, Silver Gelatin Print (Hand-Tinted), Collection of Lou Liwei

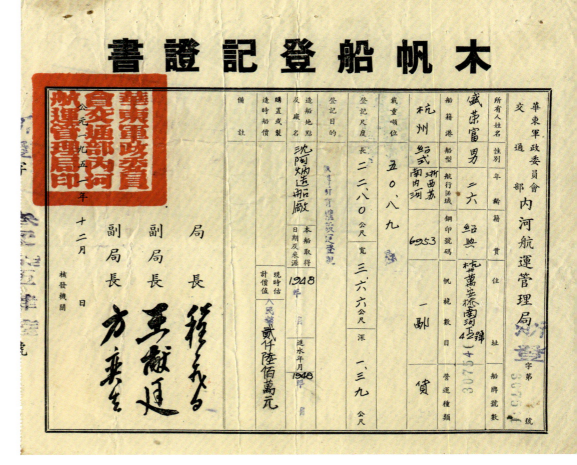

木帆船登記證書

華東軍政委員會交通部內河航運管理局

運河弓橋

对页上：**杭州香积寺边的运河。**20 世纪 10 年代，佚名摄，火棉胶照片，董桂萍收藏
对页中：**运河岸边码头。**20 世纪 10 年代，佚名摄，火棉胶照片，韩一飞收藏
对页下左：**踏春停靠。**1903 年，佚名摄，火棉胶照片，楼立伟收藏
对页下右：**临清舍利塔。**20 世纪 20 年代，佚名摄，银盐照片，张友国收藏
上：**盛荣富木帆船登记证。**1951 年，纸质证书，韩一飞收藏
下：**运河弓桥。**20 世纪 40 年代，佚名摄，彩色明信片，韩一飞收藏

Opposite Top: **Hangzhou Grand Canal near Xiangji Temple.** 1910s, Photographer Unknown, Collodion Print, Collection of Dong Guiping
Opposite Middle: **Grand Canal Wharf.** 1910s, Photographer Unknown, Collodion Print, Collection of Han Yifei
Opposite Bottom Left: **Spring Outing.** 1903, Photographer Unknown, Collodion Print, Collection of Lou Liwei
Opposite Bottom Right: **Linqing Relic Pagoda.** 1920s, Photographer Unknown, Silver Gelatin Print, Collection of Zhang Youguo
Above: **Wooden Sailboat Registration Certificate owned by Sheng Rongfu.** 1951, Paper Certificate, Collection of Han Yifei
Below: **Grand Canal Arch Bridge.** 1940s, Photographer Unknown, Color Postcard, Collection of Han Yifei

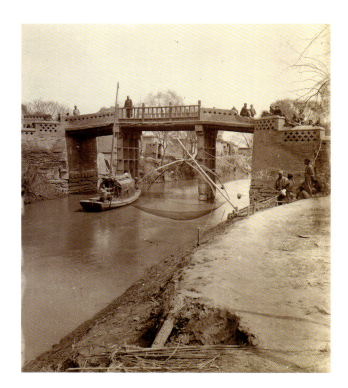

上左：**运河上的一座桥梁。** 19 世纪 90 年代，佚名摄，火棉胶照片，张友国收藏
上右：**运河上准备过闸的木船。** 19 世纪 90 年代，佚名摄，火棉胶照片，张友国收藏
　下：**苏州宝带桥。** 20 世纪 10 年代，佚名摄，火棉胶照片，高国忠收藏

Above Left: **A bridge over the Grand Canal.** 1890s, Photographer Unknown, Collodion Print, Collection of Zhang Youguo
Above Right: **Wooden boats preparing to pass through a lock on the Grand Canal.** 1890s, Photographer Unknown, Collodion Print,
    Collection of Zhang Youguo
Below: **Suzhou Baodai Bridge.** 1910s, Photographer Unknown, Collodion Print, Collection of Gao Guozhong

上：运河上航行的帆船 20 世纪 10 年代。佚名摄，火棉胶照片，韩一飞收藏
下：北方运河上的一个货运码头 20 世纪初。佚名摄，银盐纸基，张友国收藏

Above:**Sailing boats on the Grand Canal.** 1910s, Photographer Unknown, Collodion Print, Collection of Han Yifei
Below:**A cargo wharf on the Northern Grand Canal.** 1900s, Photographer Unknown, Silver Gelatin Print on Paper, Collection of Zhang Youguo

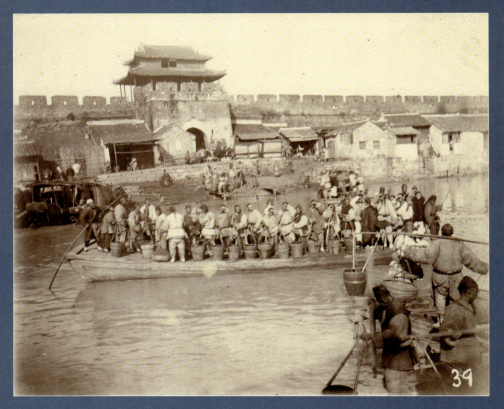

上左：**城墙外运河**。20 世纪 10 年代，佚名摄，火棉胶照片，董桂萍收藏
上中：**北运河码头**。20 世纪 10 年代，佚名摄，火棉胶照片，韩董收藏
上右：**运河渡船**。20 世纪 10 年代，佚名摄，火棉胶照片，韩董收藏
下四图：**浙东运河船翻坝过程**。20 世纪 30 年代，佚名摄，银盐照片，江建平收藏

Above Left: **Grand Canal outside the city wall.** 1910s, Photographer Unknown, Collodion Print, Collection of Dong Guiping
Above Middle: **Northern Grand Canal Wharf.** 1910s, Photographer Unknown, Collodion Print, Collection of Han Dong
Above Right: **Grand Canal Ferry.** 1910s, Photographer Unknown, Collodion Print, Collection of Han Dong
Below Four Images: **The process of a boat turning the barrier on the Zhejiang-Eastern Grand Canal.** 1930s, Photographer Unknown, Silver Gelatin Print,
　　　　　　Collection of Jiang Jianping

上：**运河船运（组照）**。20 世纪 20 年代，佚名摄，银盐照片，韩董收藏
对页：**运河嘉兴段**。20 世纪 20 年代，佚名摄，珂罗版照片，董桂萍收藏

Top: **Grand Canal Shipping (Series).** 1920s, Photographer Unknown, Silver Gelatin Print, Collection of Han Dong
Opposite: **Grand Canal in Jiaxing Section.** 1920s, Photographer Unknown, Collotype Print, Collection of Dong Guiping

Auf dem Kaiserkanal, der 540 v. Chr. begonnenen, 1400 km langen Verkehrsader durch die chinesische große Ebene

本页及对页（组照）：**南方养蚕蚕茧交易抽丝纺纱装运全过程。**20 世纪初，佚名摄，银盐照片，江建平收藏

This Page and the Opposite(Series): **The complete process of silkworms, cocoon trading, silk spinning, and shipment in the south.**
1900s, Photographer Unknown, Silver Gelatin Print, Collection of Jiang Jianping

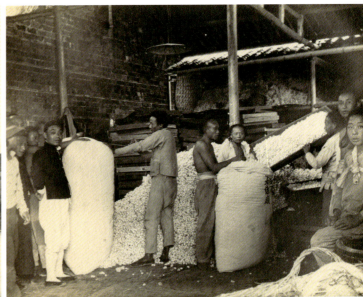

本页及对页（组照）：**大运河。**20 世纪 30 年代，佚名摄，手工上色银盐照片，江建平、韩一飞收藏

This Page and the Opposite(Series): **Grand Canal.** 1930s, Photographer Unknown, Hand-colored Silver Gelatin Prints , Collection of Jiang Jianping and Han Yifei

上： **大运河上的船工。** 20 世纪 30 年代，佚名摄，银盐照片，韩一飞收藏
对页上： **大运河上的一座桥梁。** 20 世纪 30 年代，唐纳德·曼尼摄，珂罗版照片，江建平收藏
对页下左： **大运河上的桥梁和人家。** 20 世纪 30 年代，唐纳德·曼尼摄，珂罗版照片，江建平收藏
对页下右： **河道上行驶的船只。** 20 世纪 30 年代，唐纳德·曼尼摄，珂罗版照片，张友国收藏

Above: **Boatmen on the Grand Canal.** 1930s, Photographer Unknown, Silver Gelatin Print, Collection of Han Yifei
Opposite Above: **A Bridge over the Grand Canal.** 1930s, Photographed by Donald Mennie, Collotype Print, Collection of Jiang Jianping
Opposite Below Left: **Bridges and Homes on the Grand Canal.** 1930s, Photographed by Donald Mennie, Collotype Print, Collection of Jiang Jianping
Opposite Below Right: **Boats Sailing on the River.** 1930s, Photographed by Donald Mennie, Collotype Print, Collection of Zhang Youguo

Po-Yo Bridge

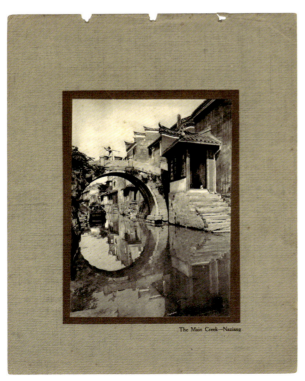

The Main Creek—Naziang

本页及对页（组照）：**大运河景观**。20 世纪 30 年代，佚名摄，银盐照片，杜晓华收藏
This Page and the Opposite (Series) : **Grand Canal Scenery.** 1930s, Photographer Unknown, Silver Gelatin Print, Collection of Du Xiaohua

上四图（组照）：**大运河景观。**20 世纪 30 年代，佚名摄，银盐照片，韩一飞收藏
　　　　对页上：**沙溪古镇市场。**1930 年前后，佚名摄，银盐照片，楼立伟收藏
　　　　对页下：**沙溪古镇。**1930 年前后，佚名摄，银盐照片，楼立伟收藏

Above Four Images (Series) : **Grand Canal Scenery.** 1930s, Photographer Unknown, Silver Gelatin Print, Collection of Han Yifei
Opposite Above: **Shaxi Ancient Town Market.** Around 1930, Photographer Unknown, Silver Gelatin Print, Collection of Lou Liwei
Opposite Below: **Shaxi Ancient Town.** Around 1930, Photographer Unknown, Silver Gelatin Print, Collection of Lou Liwei

杭州运河人家。20世纪30年代，
佚名摄，银盐照片，董桂萍收藏

Hangzhou Canal Dwellings.
1930s, Photographer Unknown,
Silver Gelatin Print, Collection of
Dong Guiping

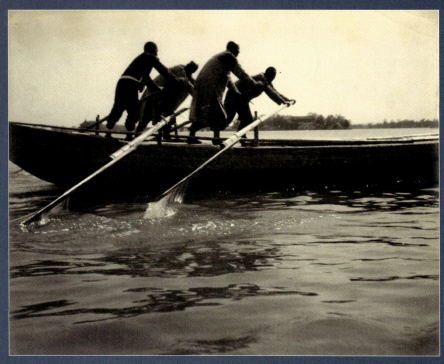

上左：**大运河上的摇橹者。**20 世纪 20 年代，佚名摄，银盐照片，韩董收藏
上右：**运河中的帆船。**20 世纪 30 年代，佚名摄，银盐照片，董桂萍收藏
下左：**运河归舟急。**1928 年，小南久一郎摄，银盐照片，楼立伟收藏
下右：**在运河内河航行的杭州湖墅民船搭载乘客。**20 世纪 30 年代，佚名摄 银盐照片，徐忠民收藏
对页：**在运河内河航行的杭州湖墅民船上的乘客。**20 世纪 30 年代，与本页右下照片来自同一私人相册，佚名摄，银盐照片，徐忠民收藏

Above Left: **Oarsmen on the Grand Canal.** 1920s, Photographer Unknown, Silver Gelatin Print, Collection of Han Dong
Above Right: **Sailboat on the Canal.** 1930s, Photographer Unknown, Silver Gelatin Print, Collection of Dong Guiping
Below Left: **Boats Returning on the Canal in a Hurry.** 1928, Photographed by Konichiro Shonan, Silver Gelatin Print, Collection of Lou Liwei
Below Right: **Hangzhou Hushu Folk Boat Carrying Passengers Navigating the Canal.** 1930s, Photographer Unknown, Silver Gelatin Print, Collection of Xu Zhongmin
Opposite: **Passengers on a Hangzhou Hushu Folk Boat Navigating the Canal.** 1930s, Photographer Unknown, From the Same Private Album as the Previous Photo, Silver Gelatin Print, Collection of Xu Zhongmin

上左：**运河支流水乡一角。**1930 年代，佚名摄，银盐照片，江建平收藏
上右：**运河岸边的牌坊群。**1930 年代，佚名摄，银盐照片，韩一飞收藏
下左：**运河边停靠的船只。**1930 年代，佚名摄，银盐照片，杜晓华收藏
下右：**苏州玉带桥桥头。**1930 年代，佚名摄，银盐照片，韩一飞收藏
对页：**运河支流上乘坐客船的女学生。**1920 年代，佚名摄，银盐照片，韩一飞收藏

Above Left: **A Corner of the Water Village on a Canal Tributary.** 1930s, Photographer Unknown, Silver Gelatin Print, Collection of Jiang Jianping
Above Right: **A Group of Memorial Archways by the Canal.** 1930s, Photographer Unknown, Silver Gelatin Print, Collection of Han Yifei
Below Left: **Boats Docked by the Canal.** 1930s, Photographer Unknown, Silver Gelatin Print, Collection of Du Xiaohua
Below Right: **The Head of Suzhou's Yudai Bridge.** 1930s, Photographer Unknown, Silver Gelatin Print, Collection of Han Yifei
Opposite: **Female Students on a Passenger Boat on a Canal Tributary.** 1920s, Photographer Unknown, Silver Gelatin Print, Collection of Han Yifei

Harbor China

对页：**繁忙的运河码头。** 20 世纪 30 年代，佚名摄，银盐照片，张友国收藏
　上：**江南水乡的村口。** 20 世纪 30 年代，佚名摄，银盐照片，杜晓华收藏

Opposite: **Busy Canal Wharf.** 1930s, Photographer Unknown, Silver Gelatin Print, Collection of Zhang Youguo
Top: **Entrance to a Village in the Jiangnan Water Towns.** 1930s, Photographer Unknown, Silver Gelatin Print, Collection of Du Xiaohua

（本页及对页照片，从左到右）
一：**北方运河渡船。**20 世纪 30 年代，佚名摄，银盐照片，韩董收藏
二：**运河岸边。**20 世纪初，佚名摄，火棉胶照片，韩一飞收藏
三：**杭州拱宸桥。**20 世纪 20 年代，留芳照相馆摄，明信片，韩一飞收藏
四：**通县附近的运河风景。**20 世纪 30 年代，佚名摄，明信片，韩一飞收藏
五：**行驶在苏州运河的帆船。**20 世纪 20 年代，唐纳德·曼尼摄，明信片，张友国收藏

(Photos from Left to Right , This Page and the Opposite)
One: **Ferry on the Northern Canal.** 1930s, Photographer Unknown, Silver Gelatin Print, Collection of Han Dong
Two: **Canal Bank.** Early 1900s, Photographer Unknown, Collodion Print, Collection of Han Yifei
Three: **Hangzhou Gongchen Bridge.** 1920s, Photographed by Liufang Studio, Postcard, Collection of Han Yifei
Four: **Canal Scenery near Tongxian County.** 1930s, Photographer Unknown, Postcard, Collection of Han Yifei
Five: **Sailboat Traveling on the Suzhou Canal.** 1920s, Photographed by Donald Mennie, Postcard, Collection of Zhang Youguo

運河風景（近縣附通）
The View of Yung-Ho
A River digged by manual labour starting from
Tung-Chow North China to Yang-Chow, South China.

On the Soochow Creek.

历史定格：名家镜头下的中国大运河

Masters of Photography: Capturing the Grand Canal

金石声
Jin Shisheng

　　中国城市规划教育的重要奠基人之一，城市规划学家、摄影艺术家。

　　1936-1937年，他在上海主编过摄影杂志《飞鹰》，共20期。他曾是中国摄影学会理事和上海市摄影家协会副主席。1961年，与刘旭沧在上海、南京、杭州、北京举办过"刘旭沧、金石声摄影艺术展览会"。1988年，他在上海美术馆举办"金石声摄影艺术展"。他在文化方面的素养是多方面的，曾为上海市文联委员。他对篆刻亦有很深的爱好和造诣。他还参与编辑了《德汉词典》，翻译过电影《贝多芬传》等。年逾古稀之时，他还在为一些摄影杂志撰文，也经常在《新民晚报》上发表一些幽默的散文，主题又多半是他的老本行——城市规划。

Jin Shisheng is one of the important founders of urban planning education in China, as well as an urban planner and photography artist.

In 1936-1937, he served as the editor-in-chief of the photography magazine *Flying Eagle* in Shanghai, with a total of 20 issues. He was once a council member of the China Photographers Association and the vice chairman of the Shanghai Photographers Association. In 1961, he and Liu Xucang held "Liu Xucang, Jin Shisheng Photography Art Exhibition" in Shanghai, Nanjing, Hangzhou, and Beijing. In 1988, another "Jin Shisheng Photography Art Exhibition" was held at Shanghai Art Museum. He had a diverse cultural background and was a committee member of Shanghai Federation of Literary and Art Circles. He had a deep passion and proficiency in seal cutting. He also participated in editing the *German-Chinese Dictionary* and translated films such as *Beethoven Biography*. Despite his advanced age, he had continued to contribute articles to photography magazines and frequently published humorous essays in *Xinmin Evening News*, most of which revolve around his expertise in urban planning.

1930 年，苏州天平山附近运河边的纤夫
Boat-trackers by the canal near Tianping Mountain in Suzhou in 1930

1953 年，嘉兴运河边行走中的规划专家钟耀华一家
In 1953, urban planning expert Zhong Yaohua and his family walking along the canal in Jiaxing

1935 年，扬州运河
The Grand Canal of Yangzhou in 1935

1935 年，拂晓时的苏州运河
The Suzhou Canal at dawn in 1935

1935 年，扬州文峰塔与古运河
The Wenfeng Pagoda and the ancient Grand Canal in Yangzhou in 1935

20 世纪 30 年代，杭州京杭运河边的妇女
Women by the Grand Canal in Hangzhou during the 1930s

1963 年，扬州新开大运河
The newly excavated Grand Canal in Yangzhou in 1963

1932 年，苏州运河上的船工在摇橹
The boatman rowing boats on the Suzhou Canal in 1932

1933 年，天平山附近运河上的运石船
Stone transport boats on the canal near Tianping Mountain in 1933

1953 年，嘉兴运河边的骑牛者与运河对岸的真如塔
In 1953, riders on oxen by the canal in Jiaxing, with the Zhenru Pagoda visible on the opposite bank

1981 年，运河运粮船的撑篙者
Polers of grain transport boats on the canal in 1981

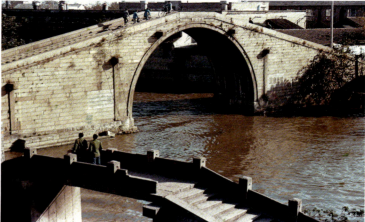

1979 年，吴门桥与水关桥
The Wumen Bridge and Shuiguan Bridge in 1979

20 世纪 20 年代，扬州运河码头
The canal docks in Yangzhou in the 1920s

吴中行
Wu Zhongxing

　　中国摄影艺术的先驱，出生于江苏省常州市天宁寺古运河畔。他所摄的运河两岸吴越文化高地的人文景观、物华风貌作品，具有诗情画意、清新自然、朴实亲切、悠然意远的艺术风格。他的艺术实践，对中国摄影与传统艺术的接榫，进而创造出独立的艺术风格，起到了不容忽视的作用。

　　吴中行的作品在 20 世纪二三十年代就闻名于世，作品《春雪》曾获 1930 年全国摄影比赛第一名。吴中行为"黑白影社"执行理事，对推动我国摄影艺术创作做出过重要的贡献。1944 年 10 月 10 日辛亥革命纪念日，他应《申报》邀请在上海举办个人摄影义展，捐款支援抗日。

　　中华人民共和国成立后，吴中行当选全国第三届文代会代表，中国摄影学会常务理事。

A pioneer in Chinese photographic art, Wu Zhongxing was born by the Fanggu Canal in Tianning Temple, Changzhou City, Jiangsu Province. His photographic works captured the humanistic landscapes of the cultural highlands along both banks of the canal in the Wu and Yue regions, showcasing the richness of culture and natural beauty. His artistic style is characterized by poetic and picturesque qualities, freshness, simplicity, and a sense of tranquility and distance. His artistic practice has bridged Chinese photography with traditional art, thereby creating an independent artistic style that played an undeniable role.

Wu Zhongxing's works were renowned in the 1920s and 1930s. His piece *Spring Snow* won first place in the 1930 National Photography Competition. He served as an executive director of the Black and White Photography Society and made significant contributions to promoting the artistic creation of photography in China. On October 10, 1944, the anniversary of the 1911 Revolution, he organized a photography charity exhibition in Shanghai at the invitation of *Shen Bao* newspaper, donating funds to support the anti-Japanese war.

After the founding of the People's Republic of China, Wu Zhongxing was elected as a representative to the Third National Congress of the China Federation of Literary and Art Circles and as a standing council member of the China Photographers Association.

牧歌。 20 世纪 60 年代，常州
Pastoral song. 1960s, Changzhou

运木。20 世纪 30 年代，常州
Transporting timber. 1930s, Changzhou

水上人家。20 世纪 30 年代，常州
Waterfront homes. 1930s, Changzhou

笔塔晨曦。20 世纪 30 年代，常州
Morning light at Bita Pagoda. 1930s, Changzhou

龙舟。20 世纪 20 年代，常州天宁寺前古运河，该运河相传为春秋吴王夫差所开
Dragon boat. 1920s, in front of Tianning Temple on the ancient canal in Changzhou. Legend has it that it was established by King Fuchai of Wu during the Spring and Autumn period

疏浚古运河。 20 世纪 50 年代，常州
Dredging of the ancient Grand Canal. 1950s, Changzhou

南来北往。 20 世纪 50 年代，常州
Northward and southward. 1950s, Changzhou

运河风貌。 20 世纪 60 年代，常州
Grand Canal scenery. 1960s, Changzhou

运河石桥。20 世纪 40 年代，常州
Canal stone bridge. 1940s, Changzhou

黄笃初
Huang Duchu

字敦补，1909 年出生于双林一家丝绸商人家庭。在外出经商的过程中，对西风东渐的摄影术深感兴趣。1927 年即购买了一架进口的布朗尼相机，利用外出经商的机会从事业余摄影，遂一发而不可收。

他的摄影作品可分为三类：一是艺术创作类，以风景和静物摄影为主，这在当时的条件下已经达到了较高的水准；二是社会风情类，表现了他强烈的存史意识；三是新闻纪录类，尤其是抗战爆发以来的新闻作品，表达了作者强烈的社会责任感和爱国精神。清光绪举人、新中国成立后为浙江省文史研究馆馆员的俞玉书，曾在《赠黄子笃初序》，对其作了高度评价。

1937 年，他举家避难苏州。全家要靠其当会计谋生，他无暇再从事摄影活动。然而，他却在几十年的风风雨雨中，一直精心保存着自己所拍摄的底片，共 559 幅。

黄笃初于 1990 年在苏州病逝，享年 82 岁。

Huang Duchu, was born in 1909 into a family of silk merchants in Shuanglin. He began learning business management from a young age. During his business travels, he developed a deep interest in Western photography techniques.In 1927, Huang Duchu purchased an imported Brouni camera. He started amateur photography during his business travels and quickly became proficient.

His photographic works can be divided into three categories: artistic creations, primarily focusing on landscape and still-life photography, reaching a high standard given the conditions of the time; social scenes, reflecting his strong sense of historical consciousness; and news documentation, particularly capturing the atrocities and devastation committed by the Japanese aggressors since the outbreak of the Anti-Japanese War, revealing the author's humanistic awareness and strong sense of social responsibility. Yu Yushu, a Jinshi scholar in the Qing dynasty and a researcher at the Zhejiang Provincial Research Institute for Culture and History after the liberation, wrote a preface for Huang Duchu, highly praising his works.

In 1937, Huang Duchu and his family sought refuge in Suzhou. He had to support his family by working as an accountant, leaving him no time for photography. However, he meticulously preserved the negatives of his photographs over the decades, totaling 559 pieces.

Huang Duchu passed away in Suzhou in 1990 at the age of 82.

善琏八字桥。 20 世纪 30 年代，湖州
Shanlian Bazhi Bridge. 1930s, Huzhou

双林墨浪河畔。1930 年代，湖州
Shuanglin Molang Riverside. 1930s, Huzhou

大虹桥、小虹桥和还金亭。1930 年代，湖州
Dahong Bridge, Xiaohong Bridge, and Huanjin Pavilion. 1930s, Huzhou

双林镇文昌阁。1929 年，湖州
Wenchang Pavilion in Shuanglin Town. 1929, Huzhou

西湖博览会大门入口。 1929 年，杭州
Entrance Gate of the West Lake Exposition. 1929, Hangzhou

为西湖博览会专门搭建的桥。 1929 年，杭州
Bridge Specially Built for the West Lake Exposition. 1929, Hangzhou

鸟瞰西湖。 1930 年代，杭州
Aerial View of West Lake. 1930s, Hangzhou

谢伟洪
Xie Weihong

1955 年 3 月生，浙江省摄影家协会会员，杭州市临平区摄影家协会名誉主席。

1980 年从事摄影创作至今，有百余幅作品在国际、国内各种摄影比赛中获奖，其中《视而不见》获上海第 11 届国际影赛入选奖，《胶片里的八十年代》摄影作品在大理国际摄影节、平遥国际摄影节、杭州第五届市民摄影节上展出。2014 年被快拍网评为首届运河十佳摄影师。2017 年出版《那年的塘栖》摄影画册，在《中国摄影》《大众摄影》《摄影世界》杂志和《人民摄影》报等全国性报刊发表作品 500 多幅。

Born in March 1955, Xie Weihong is a member of Zhejiang Photographers Association and the Honorary Chairman of Linping District Photographers Association in Hangzhou.

Since starting his photography career in 1980, he has won awards in various international and domestic photography competitions with over a hundred works. Among them, *Seeing without Seeing* won the selection award at the 11th Shanghai International Photography Contest. His series *The 1980s in Film* was exhibited at Dali International Photography Festival, Pingyao International Photography Festival, and the 5th Hangzhou Citizens Photography Festival. In 2014, he was named one of the top ten photographers along the Grand Canal by Kuai Pai Net. In 2017, he published a photography album titled *Those Years in Tangqi* and his works have been published in national newspapers and magazines such as *Chinese Photography*, *Popular Photography*, *Photography World* and *People's Photography* with over 500 images.

运河上的手拉渡船已成为历史。1996 年 5 月，临平亭趾
Hand-pulled ferry boats on the Grand Canal have become history. Tingzhi Town in Linping, May 1996

20 世纪 80 年代，在塘栖丁山河经常可以看到的摇着小船走亲戚的场景。1985 年 10 月，塘栖
This scene of rowing boats for social visits was common in Dingshan River, Tangqi, during the 1980s. Tangqi, October 1985

20 世纪 70 年代末，京杭大运河崇贤三家村渡口每天都很繁忙。运河南岸的农民要去运河北岸卖菜、种田都会选择坐船。一条小船能渡 20 多人。1978 年 12 月，崇贤三家村

In the late 1970s, the Chongxian Sajia Village ferry crossing on the Beijing-Hangzhou Grand Canal was bustling every day. Farmers from south bank had to cross to the north bank to sell vegetables or tend to their fields, often opting for boat travel. Each small boat could ferry more than 20 people. Chongxian Sajia Village,December 1978

20 世纪 80 年代，家里有一台"西湖牌"黑白电视机，是让人羡慕的事。1988 年 11 月，塘栖广济桥
In the 1980s, having a West Lake brand black and white television at home was something that made others envious. Guangji Bridge in Tangqi, November 1988

京杭大运河水上运输繁忙，一条长龙拖船可以拖几百吨货物。1992 年 4 月，塘栖
The water transportation on the Beijing-Hangzhou Grand Canal was bustling, with a long dragon-towed boat capable of towing hundreds of tons of cargo. Tangqi, April 1992

吴家弄是当时塘栖比较有特色的一条老巷子，现在这里已建成商品房。1987 年 8 月，塘栖吴家弄
Wujia Lane was a distinctive old alley in Tangqi at that time. It has now been developed into commercial housing. Wujia Lane in Tangqi, August 1987

清代学者俞樾居住过的史家埭。1995 年 10 月，临平史家埭
Shijiadai, where the Qing Dynasty scholar Yu Yue once lived. Shijiadai in Linping,October 1995

江南水乡的黄梅天和雷阵雨，是两大雨天的特色：黄梅天雨下个没完没了，下得人心烦；夏天
的雷阵雨，往往下得人措手不及，还有东边太阳西边雨的景色。1990 年 8 月，塘栖八字桥埭
The yellow plum rain and thunderstorms are two characteristic rainy days in the water towns of Jiangnan. The endless drizzle during the
yellow plum rain season often becomes vexing. In summer, thunderstorms often catch you off guard, and the scenery of the sun shining
brightly in the east while it rains in the west is not uncommon. Tangqi's Baziqiao Dock,August 1990

沈 英
Shen Ying

生于四川成都，1949 年自愿参加中国人民解放军二野十一军文工团，1950 年编为海军青岛基地文工团。1958 年转业，先后任沧州群艺馆辅导干部、海河文艺宣传队队长等职务。1974 年调沧州地委宣传部工作，任外宣局科长，负责对外宣传工作，1989 年退休。1988 年，沈英牵头成立全国第一个女性摄影组织——河北省女摄影家协会，并担任主席。

沈英在摄影事业上取得了重大成就，在沧州对外宣传上做出了突出贡献，曾创办《沧州新闻》图片报，筹办数十场大型摄影展，为沧州改革开放鸣锣开道。其摄影作品入选第十四届、十五届、十七届全国摄影艺术展览，有 500 多幅（次）被各类报刊采用，并被选送到美国、日本、英国、德国、朝鲜、比利时等国的国际影展展出。

Born in Chengdu, Sichuan Province, Shen Ying voluntarily joined the 11th Army Cultural Troupe of the Chinese People's Liberation Army in 1949. In 1950, she was assigned to the Navy Qingdao Base Cultural Troupe. In 1958, she transferred to civilian work, serving successively as an instructional cadre at Cangzhou Art Gallery and as the captain of Haihe Art Propaganda Team. In 1974, she was transferred to work at Cangzhou Municipal Committee's Publicity Department, where she served as the head of the External Publicity Bureau, responsible for foreign publicity work. She retired in 1989.In 1988, Shen Ying took the lead in establishing the first national women's photography organization in China—Hebei Women Photographers Association—and served as its chairperson.

Shen Ying achieved significant accomplishments in the field of photography and made outstanding contributions to external Publicity in Cangzhou. She founded *Cangzhou News* photo newspaper, organized dozens of large-scale photography exhibitions, and paved the way for Cangzhou's reform and opening up. Her photographic works were selected for the 14th, 15th, and 17th National Photographic Art Exhibitions, with over 500 pieces being used by various newspapers and magazines. Her works were also selected for exhibitions in international film festivals in countries including the United States, Japan, the United Kingdom, Germany, North Korea, and Belgium.

吴桥杂技 #8，20 世纪 80 年代
Wuqiao Acrobatics #18, Wuqiao County, City, 1980s

吴桥杂技 #1，20 世纪 80 年代
Wuqiao Acrobatics #1，Wuqiao County, City, 1980s

吴桥杂技 #15，20 世纪 80 年代
Wuqiao Acrobatics #15，Wuqiao County, City, 1980s

悠悠运河古道，流淌着千年杂技文化。

吴桥，杂技历史悠久、源远流长，是中国杂技艺术的发祥地，是世界杂技的摇篮。吴桥民间杂技更具有鲜明的特色，其艺术风格粗犷豪放，生活气息浓郁，已成为我国艺苑中一簇绚丽的奇葩。（这里展示的是已故摄影家沈英老师在 20 世纪 80 年代初拍摄的吴桥民间杂技）

The ancient canal pathway flows, carrying with it a millennium of acrobatic culture.

Wuqiao, with its long and profound history of acrobatics, is the birthplace of Chinese acrobatic art and the cradle of world acrobatics. Folk acrobatics in Wuqiao possess even more distinctive characteristics, with a bold and rugged artistic style and a rich atmosphere of daily life. It has become a dazzling gem in the garden of Chinese art. (Displayed here are folk acrobatics in Wuqiao captured by the late photographer, Shen Ying, in the early 1980s.)

吴桥杂技 #12，20 世纪 80 年代
Wuqiao Acrobatics #12, Wuqiao County, City, 1980s

吴桥杂技 #7，20 世纪 80 年代
Wuqiao Acrobatics #7, Wuqiao County, City, 1980s

吴桥杂技 #6，20 世纪 80 年代
Wuqiao Acrobatics #6，Wuqiao County, City, 1980s

吴桥杂技 #2，20 世纪 80 年代
Wuqiao Acrobatics #2，Wuqiao County, City, 1980s

吴桥杂技 #10, 20 世纪 80 年代
Wuqiao Acrobatics #10, Wuqiao County, City, 1980s

汤德胜
Tang Desheng

1948 年生，江苏武进人，摄影家。

1965 年至 1971 年任部队摄影记者，1971 年至 2021 年 9 月在武进区文化局从事专业摄影艺术创作。为国家一级美术师。曾任中国摄影家协会第三、第四、第五届理事，中国华侨摄影学会常务理事，江苏省摄协副主席。40 多年来，他始终坚持深入生活、心装群众、情系百姓，用镜头谱写他们的人生精彩，收获了许多精品佳作：《公社幼儿园》《大炼钢铁》等 100 多幅摄影作品入选多届"国展"和"国际影展"，并在国际、国内的摄影作品展中多次获得过金、银、铜牌奖。

Born in 1948, Tang Desheng is from Wujin, Jiangsu Province, and is a photographer.

From 1965 to 1971, he served as a military photographer. From 1971 until September 2021, he worked in the Cultural Bureau of Wujin District, specializing in professional photographic art creation. He holds the title of National First-Class Artist. He served as a director of China Photographers Association during the third, fourth, and fifth sessions, and is an executive director of China Society of Overseas Chinese Photographers and vice chairman of Jiangsu Photographers Association. For over 40 years, he has consistently delved into people's lives, empathized with the masses, and connected with the people's emotions. Through his lens, he has documented the splendid lives of the people, producing many outstanding works. Over 100 of his photographs, such as *Commune Kindergarten* and *Steel Smelting*, have been selected for National Photographic Art Exhibition and international exhibitions, winning gold, silver, and bronze awards in numerous photography exhibitions both domestically and internationally.

点红。1981 年，武进马巷公社陆家塘生产队
Dotting red,Lujiatang Production Brigade, Maxiang Commune, Wujin District,1981

百万农民疏浚大运河。1970 年，苏浙段运河

Millions of farmers dredged the Grand Canal, the section of the Grand Canal spanning Jiangsu and Zhejiang provinces,1970

收工回家的路上。1970 年，江苏
On the way home from work, Jiangsu Province,1970

插秧季节。1968 年，苏北
Transplanting rice seedlings season, Northern Jiangsu,1968

运河上的大白菜。1971 年，丹阳县
Cabbages on the canal, Danyangxian,1971

刘世昭
Liu Shizhao

1948 年 12 月 6 日生于四川省成都市，"四月影会"重要成员，知名摄影家，中国摄影家协会会员，世界华人摄影学会会员。

1979 年起担任《人民中国》杂志摄影记者。1981 年从北京出发骑单车万里行程采访拍摄京杭大运河，留下许多珍贵照片。时隔 35 年，68 岁的刘世昭依然壮心不已，再次出发单骑拍摄京杭大运河，旨在重塑运河影像史。数十年来，作品多次获得国家级奖项，出版有《流淌的史诗》《徒步三峡》等。

Born on December 6, 1948, in Chengdu, Sichuan Province, Liu Shizhao is a prominent member of April Photography Society and a well-known photographer. He is a member of China Photographers Association and World Chinese Photography Society.

Since 1979, he has served as a photojournalist for *People's China* magazine. In 1981, he embarked on a solo bicycle journey from Beijing to document the Beijing-Hangzhou Grand Canal, capturing many precious photographs. At the age of 68, Liu Shizhao embarked on another solo expedition to photograph the Beijing-Hangzhou Grand Canal, aiming to reshape the visual history of the canal. Over the decades, his works have won numerous national awards, and he has published books such as *The Epic of Flowing Waves* and *Hiking the Three Gorges*.

运河边的客运码头。1982 年，嘉兴
Passenger Terminal by the Canal, Jiaxing City, 1982

京杭大运河上施桥船闸外等待过闸的船队。1982 年，扬州
Fleet waiting outside Shiqiao Lock on the Grand Canal, Yangzhou City, 1982

京杭大运河边的船码头和河中的唐代镇国寺塔。1982 年，高邮
A boat dock on the Grand Canal and the Zhenguosi Pagoda built in Tang Dynasty, Gaoyou, 1982

京杭大运河上施桥船闸内过闸的船队。1982 年，扬州
Fleet passing through Shiqiao Lock on the Grand Canal, Yangzhou City, 1982

生活在运河边。20 世纪 80 年代，无锡
Life on the Grand Canal，Wuxi, 1980s

运河上的帆船和河中心的唐代镇国寺塔。1982 年，高邮
Sailboats on the Grand Canal with the Zhenguosi Pagoda built in the Tang Dynasty in the center of the river,Gaoyou,1982

兴济镇骡马集市。1981 年，河北青县
Mule and Horse Market in Xingji Town, Qingxian County, Hebei Province,1981

临平塘栖镇京杭大运河上的广济长桥。1982 年，杭州
Guangji Bridge on the Grand Canal in Tangqi Town, Linping District, Hangzhou,1982

穿城而过的京杭大运河。1982 年，常州
The Grand Canal passing through the city, Changzhou, 1982

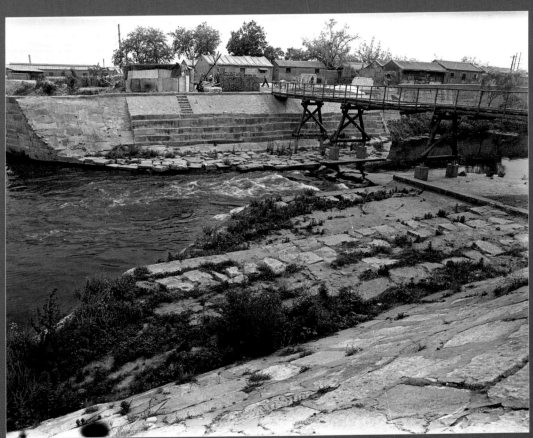

通惠河上的庆丰闸遗址。1981 年，北京
Remains of the Qingfeng Lock on the Tonghui River, Beijing, 1981

吴国方
Wu Guofang

　　浙江日报报业集团图片中心高级记者（退休），中国新闻摄影学会会员，中国摄影家协会会员。

　　20 世纪 70 年代爱上摄影，1993 年从机关调到《经济生活报》，2000 年为《今日早报》摄影部负责人。2002-2005 年为浙江在线网站《世纪摄影》频道主持。2012 年从浙江日报报业集团图片中心退休。1985-2015 年，任杭州市摄协理事、副秘书长。2010-2015 年，任浙江省摄影家协会理事。1999-2002 年连续四年获评《人民日报》"华东新闻摄影十佳"，2007 年获评杭州市第三届摄影"十佳"，2009 年获评 1979-2009 年浙江省优秀摄影家。

A retired senior journalist from Zhejiang Daily Press Group's Photo Center, member of Photojournalist Society of China, and member of China Photographers Association.

He developed a passion for photography in the 1970s. In 1993, he transferred from a government office to *Economic Life Daily*, and in 2000, he became the head of the photography department at *Today Morning News*. From 2002 to 2005, he hosted the "Century Photography" channel on Zhejiang Online website. He retired from Zhejiang Daily Press Group's Photo Center in 2012. From 1985 to 2015, he served as a director and deputy secretary-general of Hangzhou Photographers Association. From 2010 to 2015, he served as a director of Zhejiang Photographers Association. For four consecutive years from 1999 to 2002, he was named one of the Top Ten News Photographers in East China by the *People's Daily*. In 2007, he was awarded as one of the Top Ten Photographers in Hangzhou, and in 2009, he was recognized as an Outstanding Photographer in Zhejiang from 1979 to 2009.

八卦田闸口电厂。1980 年
Eight Diagrams Zhakou Power Plant,1980

疏浚中河。1997 年，杭州
Dredging of the Zhong River. Hangzhou, 1997

文龙巷小学的学生在中河边劳动。1987 年，杭州
Students from Wenlongxiang Primary School working by the Zhong River. Hangzhou, 1987

庆春路改造。1993 年，杭州
Renovation of Qingchun Road. Hangzhou, 1993

中河建设中。1985 年，杭州
Construction ongoing at the Zhong River. Hangzhou, 1985

三堡二线船闸开通。1996 年，杭州
The opening of the second line of locks in Sanbao. Hangzhou, 1996

艮山门蔬菜批发市场后的运河菜船，1993 年，杭州
Canal vegetable boat behind the Genshanmen Vegetable Wholesale Market. Hangzhou, 1993

复兴路改造时的中河。1995 年，杭州
The Zhong River during the renovation of Fuxing Road. Hangzhou, 1995

航拍中河胡雪岩故居和德寿宫。2023 年，杭州
Aerial view of the former residence of Hu Xueyan and Deshou Palace on the Zhong River. Hangzhou, 2023

吴 德
Wu De

　　中国摄影家协会会员，浙江省摄影家协会理事，浙江省企业家摄影协会副主席。

　　1980 年开始从事摄影创作。《极境的魅力》《三色阶》《吴德的天地》《诗路墨韵》等代表作先后在《中国摄影报》《人民摄影》报等国家级媒体平台发表；《一代芳华》获第 19 届浙江省摄影艺术展览纪录类金质典藏，并在《中国摄影》杂志发表；《无极》获三江源国际摄影节大展奖；《幸福之水》获第 3 届摄影无疆界世界杯国际摄影双年展金牌、第 12 届上海国际摄影艺术展览铜奖等。策展"时·空"摄影师八人联展，入选 2019 丽水摄影节。出版《极色》《虞山舜水》《芳华》等摄影著作。创立雅图时空摄影艺术馆、曹娥江诗路摄影驿站、"芳华"上棉记忆影像馆，先后策展举办摄影等艺术展览 30 余次。

A member of China Photographers Association, director of Zhejiang Photographers Association, and vice chairman of Zhejiang Entrepreneurs Photographers Association.

He began his photography career in 1980. His representative works such as *Charm of the Extreme*, *Three Tones*, *Wu De's World*, *Poetry Road Ink Rhyme* and others have been published in national media platforms such as *China Photo Press* and *People's Photography*. *A Generation of Youth* won the gold collection of the 19th Provincial Exhibition in the documentary category and was published in *Chinese Photography* magazine. *Infinite* won the Grand Exhibition Award at the Sanjiangyuan International Photography Festival; "Waters of Happiness" won the gold medal at the 3rd Photography Without Borders World Cup International Photography Biennial and the bronze award at the 12th Shanghai International Photography Art Exhibition, etc. He curated the exhibition "Time · Space" with eight photographers, which was selected for the 2019 Lishui Photography Festival. He authored and published several photography monographs such as *Extreme Colors*, *Yushan and Shunshui*, and *A Generation of Youth*. He founded the Seattle Time-Space Photography Art Museum, Cao'e River Poetry Road Photography Station, and "A Generation of Youth" Memory in Shangyu Cotton Textile Company Image Museum, and curated more than 30 art exhibitions including photography.

曹娥江上的埠头。1991 年
The wharf on Cao'e River, 1991

去对岸劳作，渡轮是当时必备的交通工具。1982 年
Crossing to work on the opposite bank, ferries were essential means of transportation at that time, 1982

手拉车搬运嫁妆的队伍，在田间形成了一道风景。1985 年
The procession of hand-pul'ed carts carrying dowries formed a picturesque scene in the fields, 1985

造新房上梁时要讨个好彩头。1990 年
When building a new house and putting up the ridge beam, it's important to seek good luck, 1990

民间艺人在冬季文艺大会上表演。1995 年
Folk artists performing during a winter cultural gala, 1995

酒坛上的戏迷。1994 年
Fans of traditional opera gathered around a wine barrel,1994

娃哈哈"双宝素"随着人群回家。1995 年
The "Wa Ha Ha" Double Treasure Drink accompanies
the crowd on their way home, 1995

排排坐来看新娘的儿童。1985 年
Children sitting in rows to watch the bride,1985

络绎不绝的路人，在层层叠叠的沙包上艰难通行。1991 年
A continuous stream of pedestrians, navigating through layers of sandbags with difficulty, 1991

割草是放学后的必备"功课"。1983 年
Mowing the grass was a necessary "homework" after school, 1983

贴满明星画报的堂前，打麦、管小孩两不误。1985 年
In front of the hall, covered with celebrity magazines, enjoying both threshing the wheat and watching small figures, 1985

打油菜籽，我们乐在其中。1985 年
Extracting rapeseed oil, we find joy in the process, 1985

28 寸的"凤凰牌"重磅自行车是当时重要的运输工具。1983 年
The 28-inch Phoenix brand heavyweight bicycle was an important means of transportation at that time, 1983

严新荣
Yan Xinrong

中国摄影家协会会员，英国皇家摄影学会会员，浙江省摄影艺术学会副主席，嘉兴市摄影家协会专家委员。

对摄影艺术有不懈的追求，曾三进西藏摄影创作。拍摄世界文化遗产大运河系列专题，致力于"黑白江南"系列专题摄影研究，用简单而本真的"黑白"颜色和语言诠释中国式的唯美，探索中华文化的历史本色，演绎江南运河文化的精神。

A member of China Photographers Association and Royal Photographic Society of Britain, Yan Xinrong serves as the vice chairman of Zhejiang Photography Art Association and an expert member of Jiaxing Photographers Association.

With an unyielding pursuit of photographic art, Yan Xinrong has embarked on three photographic expeditions to Tibet. He has undertaken a series of thematic photography projects on the Great Canal, a UNESCO World Heritage Site, and has been dedicated to researching photography through the "Black and White Jiangnan" series. Through the simple yet genuine use of black and white colors and language, he interprets the Chinese aesthetic, exploring the enhancement of the historical essence of Chinese culture and unraveling the spirit of Jiangnan Canal culture.

运河·母亲。2000 年，王江泾长虹桥
Canal: Mother . Wangjiangjing Changhong Bridge, 2000

运河之水天上来。20 世纪 80 年代，长安塘运河
The Water of the Canal Comes from the Sky. Chang'an Pond section of the canal, 1980s

依水而居自然村。20 世纪 80 年代，梧桐运河段支流
Naturally Villages along the Water. a tributary section of the canal in the Wutong area,1980s

运河集市。20 世纪 70 年代，崇福春风桥堍
Canal market. Chongfu Chunfeng Bridge Wharf, 1970s

黄金水道。20 世纪 90 年代，羔羊乡运河段
Golden waterway. the section of the canal in Gaoyang Township, 1990s

交公粮。20 世纪 70 年代，崇福南门粮库
Delivering Public Grain. Chongfu South Gate Granary, 1970s

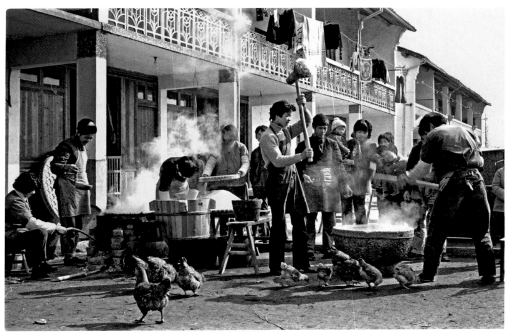

过春节打年糕。20 世纪 80 年代，留良乡
Making rice cakes for the Spring Festival, rural areas of Liuliang Township,1980s

含山庙会踏白船。20 世纪 70 年代，运河含山段
Attending the Hanshan Temple Fair and Stepping onto White Boats, the Hanshan section of the canal, 1970s

近水楼台先得鱼。20 世纪 90 年代，乌镇东栅
Near the water's edge, one gets fish first. East Area of Wuzhen, 1990s

隔河观戏。20 世纪 90 年代，古镇西塘
Watching opera across the river. Xitang Ancient Town, 1990s

船上看大戏。20 世纪 80 年代，绍兴运河段
Watching opera on board. the section of the canal in Shaoxing, 1980s

渔歌唱晚。20 世纪 90 年代，西塘古镇
Singing Fishermen's Songs at Dusk. Xitang Ancient Town, 1990s

王芯克
Wang Xinke

浙江省摄影家协会副主席，杭州市摄影艺术学会主席，高级记者，原《青年时报》副总编。中国摄影金像奖、中国新闻奖、浙江省飘萍奖获得者，被授予浙江省优秀摄影家，全国地市报摄影"十杰"记者等称号。

Vice Chairman of Zhejiang Photographers Association, Chairman of Hangzhou Photography Art Society, senior journalist, and former deputy editor-in-chief of *Youth Times*, has received numerous awards, including the Golden Statue Award for China Photography, the China Journalism Award, Zhejiang Piao Ping Award, Zhejiang Outstanding Photographer Award, and the National Top Ten Journalists in City-Level Newspaper Photography.

运河杭州段。2023 年 5 月（上），1995 年 4 月（下），艮山门
The Hangzhou section of the Grand Canal, Genshanmen, May 2023 (above), April 1995 (below)

运河杭州段。2022 年 11 月（上），1998 年 11 月（下），河罕上码头
The Hangzhou section of the Grand Canal, Hehan Shang Wharf,
November 2022 (above), November 1998 (below)

运河杭州段。2014 年 6 月（上），1998 年 11 月（下），拱宸桥
The Hangzhou section of the Grand Canal, Gongchen Bridge,
June 2014 (above), November 1998 (below)

运河杭州段。2021 年 9 月（上），2005 年 9 月（下），笕杭线运河桥
The Hangzhou section of the Grand Canal, Jianhang Canal Bridge, September 2021 (above), September 2005 (below)

葛 华
Ge Hua

　　江苏淮安人，毕业于武汉大学新闻系摄影专业。现为江苏省淮安市楚州区文化馆副馆长，副研究馆员。中国摄影家协会会员，江苏省艺术摄影学会理事，江苏省淮安市楚州区摄影家协会主席。

　　1992年获省文化厅、省电视台举办的"江苏省首届群文干部知识技能竞赛"摄影项第3名。1996年、1998年连续两届被淮安市委、市政府授予"淮安市优秀知识分子"称号。2000年被淮安市人民政府授予"五一劳动奖章"。

A native of Huai'an, Jiangsu Province, Ge Hua graduated from the photography department of the School of Journalism at Wuhan University. He currently serves as the deputy director and associate researcher of the Cultural Center of Chuzhou District, Huai'an City, Jiangsu Province. He is a member of China Photographers Association and a director of Jiangsu Art Photography Society. Additionally, he is the Chairman of Chuzhou District Photographers Association in Huai'an City, Jiangsu Province.

In 1992, he ranked third in the photography category of the "First Jiangsu Province Mass Cultural Cadres Knowledge and Skills Competition" held by the Provincial Department of Culture and the Provincial Television Station. In 1996 and 1998, he was consecutively awarded the title of "Outstanding Intellectual of Huai'an City" by Huai'an Municipal Committee and Government. In 2000, he was awarded the "May 1st Labor Medal" by Huai'an Municipal People's Government.

临近春节，在外打工的农民和在外读书的学子陆续回家过年。2018 年 2 月 4 日，泾河渡口
With the Spring Festival approaching, migrant workers returning home and students studying away from home are gradually returning home for the Lunar New Year.Jinghe Ferry Crossing,February 4, 2018

渡口边的母女三人。2018年2月4日，泾河渡口
A mother and her two daughters by the ferry crossing.Jinghe Ferry Crossing,February 4, 2018

有时渡船刚起动便会遇上正在急速行驶的货船，这时渡船只能返回码头，等待货船通过后再起动。2018 年 2 月 13 日，泾河渡口
Sometimes just as the ferry starts moving, it encounters a cargo ship traveling at high speed. In such cases, the ferry has to return to the dock and wait for the cargo ship to pass before it can resume its journey.Jinghe Ferry Crossing. Sometimes,February 13, 2018

一块水泥做的牌子竖立在路边，告诉过河的人
渡口在树林里面。2018 年 2 月 4 日，袁庄渡口

A cement sign stands by the roadside, indicating to travelers that the
ferry crossing is located within the grove of trees.Yuanzhuang Ferry
Crossing,February 4, 2018

待渡亭的窗口像一个画框，将摆渡的时空定格。
2015 年 4 月 25 日，陈庄渡口

The window of the waiting pavilion resembles a picture frame,
capturing the passage of time during the ferry crossing.
Chenzhuang Ferry Crossing,April 25, 2015

两名骑摩托车的时尚女性在待渡亭旁，一边等待摆渡，一边看手机。2015 年 4 月 11 日，林平渡口
Two stylish women riding motorcycles wait by the waiting pavilion, simultaneously waiting for the ferry and looking at their phones.Linping Ferry Crossing,April 11, 2015

乘客正在登上苏淮渡 519 号渡船。2018 年 2 月 4 日，泾河渡口
Passengers are boarding the ferry named "Su Huai Ferry No. 519".Jinghe Ferry Crossing,February 4, 2018

春节将至，渡口一片忙碌景象。2018 年 2 月 4 日，泾河渡口
With the Spring Festival approaching, the ferry crossing is bustling with activity.Jinghe Ferry Crossing.,February 4, 2018

苏淮渡 519 渡船上的渡工曹长青 65 岁，开渡船已 40 多年了。2019 年 3 月 10 日，泾河渡口
Cao Changqing, 65 years old this year, works as a ferryman on Su Huai Ferry No. 519. He has been operating ferries for over 40 years.Jinghe Ferry Crossing,March 10, 2019

渡船上的儿童望着运河水若有所思。2019 年 3 月 10 日，泾河渡口
A child on the ferry gazes thoughtfully at the water of the canal.Jinghe Ferry Crossing,March 10, 2019

时代新声：摄影家心目中的现代大运河

Modern Grand Canal through the Lens of Photographers

日出东方 泰安，商和兰
Sunrise in the East. Taian, Shang Helan

鸟类乐园 洛阳，张良
Bird park. Luoyang, Zhang Liang

洛浦晨雾 洛阳，周胜利
Morning mist in Luopu. Luoyang, Zhou Shengli

金色家园 镇江，罗秀龙
Golden home. Zhenjiang, Luo Xiulong

潮起钱塘江时代（组照）杭州，邹洁
The Era when the tide rises in the Qiantang River (Series). Hangzhou, Zou Jie

中国龙 洛阳，朱雨云
Chinese dragon, Luoyang, Zhu Yuyun

黄金水道　杭州，张友国
Golden waterway. Hangzhou, Zhang Youguo

醉美宁波港 宁波，余文华
Beautiful Ningbo Port. Ningbo, Yu Wenhua

龙越 天津，季红伟
Jumping into the river. Tianjin, Ji Hongwei

杭州运河全景图　杭州，邹洁
Panoramic view of Hangzhou Canal. Hangzhou, Zou Jie

龙门伊阙关，客家先民南迁必经之路　洛阳，高均海
Longmen Yique Pass, the essential route for Hakka ancestors' southward migration. Luoyang, Gao Junhai

海河入海口 天津，王广荣
Mouth of the Haihe River. Tianjin, Wang Guangrong

魅力运河（组照）杭州，朱亮亮
Charming canal(Series). Hangzhou, Zhu Liangliang

南湖胜境 泰安，潘景臣
Scenic beauty of Nanhu. Taian, Pan Jingchen

隋唐运河盛景 洛阳，高均海
Grand scenery of the Sui and Tang Grand Canal. Luoyang, Gao Junhai

运河边的学校（组照） 杭州，魏春
School by the Canal(Series). Hangzhou, Wei Chun

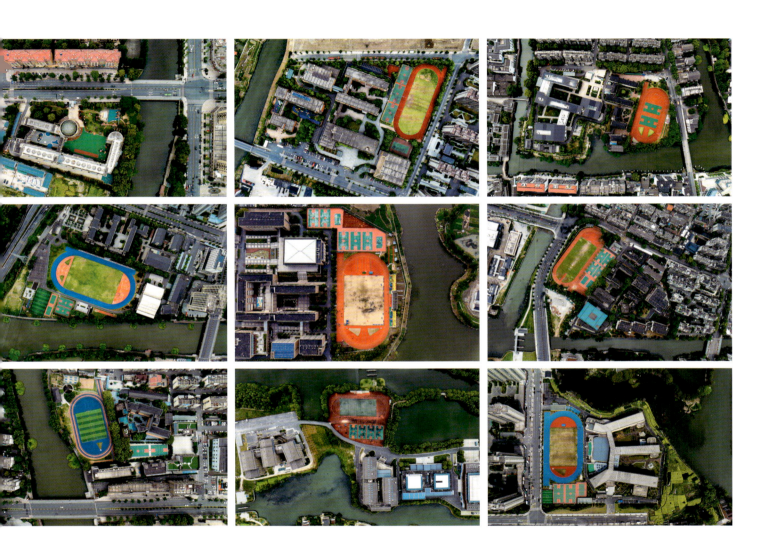

		2	3	4
1		5	6	7
		8	9	10

1. 运河幼儿园 - Canal Kindergarten
2. 塘栖第二幼儿园 - Tangqi Second Kindergarten
3. 塘栖第二小学 - Tangqi Second Elementary School
4. 杭州塘栖第一小学 - Hangzhou Tangqi First Elementary School
5. 杭州市塘栖第三中学 - Hangzhou Tangqi Third Middle School
6. 运河中学 - Canal Middle School
7. 塘栖职业高级中学 - Tangqi Vocational High School
8. 杭州塘栖第三小学 - Hangzhou Tangqi Third Elementary School
9. 杭州市第四机械技工学校 - Hangzhou Fourth Mechanical Technical School
10. 运河小学 - Canal Elementary School

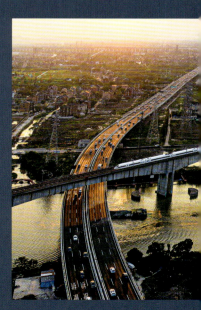

运河沿岸的杭州影像　杭州，吴海平
Images of Hangzhou Along the Canal(Series). Hangzhou, Wu Haiping

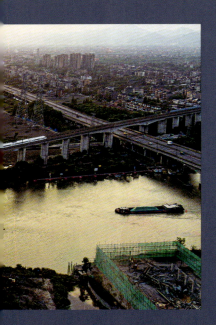

越水长卷（组照） 绍兴，王杨钢
Scroll of Yue Water(Series). Shaoxing, Wang Yanggang

雪浴古郡（组照）沧州，王剑江
The ancient country bathing in snow(Series). Cangzhou, Wang Jianjiang

冰上游龙 北京，1995，王生生
Ice dragon on the river . Beijing, 1995, Wang Shengsheng

周末 杭州，孙加英
Weekend. Hangzhou, Sun Jiaying

我眼中的运河水乡 杭州，郑水兴
Impressions of the water village by the Canal in my eyes. Hangzhou, Zheng Shuixing

生活在运河边的人 杭州，邵赴明
People living by the Canal. Hangzhou, Shao Fuming

北京通州西海子
Xihaizi Park in Tongzhou, Beijing

第 168-173 页：北京的运河（组照） 季红伟
Pages 168-173: **The Beijing Canal (Series)**. Ji Hongwei

北京通州大稿村
Dagao Village in Tongzhou, Beijing

北京昌平运河源头白浮泉
Baifu Spring at the source of the Canal in Changping Beijing

北京通州白庙
Baimiao Temple in Tongzhou,Beijing

北京通州运河森林公园
Canal Forest Park in Tongzhou,Beijing

北京通州燃灯塔
Lighthouse Pagoda in Tongzhou,Beijing

北京通州雪中的千荷泻露桥
The Thousand Dewdrops Bridge in snowy Tongzhou, Beijing

第 174-177 页：**淮安日常（组照）**朱晓兵
Pages 174-177：**Huai'an daily life (Series)**. Zhu Xiaobing

第 178-183 页: **桥头记忆（组照）** 杭州，杨志坚
Pages 178-183: **Memories at the bridgehead (Series)**. Hangzhou, Yang Zhijian

姑婆桥 Gupo Bridge

前溪西桥 Qianxi West Bridge

石灰桥 Lime Bridge

第 184-187 页：**古桥（组照）** 杭州，宋峤
Pages 184-187：**Ancient bridge, Hangzhou (Series).** Hangzhou, Song Qiao

胭脂桥 Yanzhi Bridge

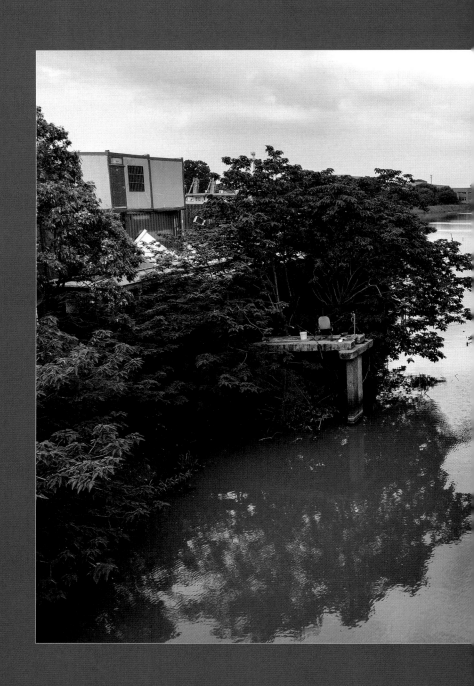

余库桥 Yuku Bridge

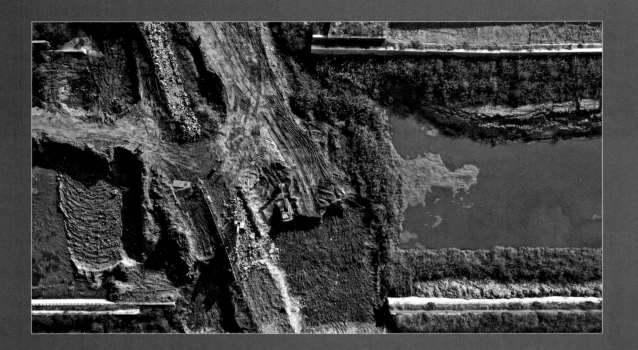

痕迹（组照） 京杭运河杭州段二通道，阳益平
Traces (Series). second channel of the Hangzhou section of the Grand Canal, Yang Yiping

德州洪水过后运河里的树
The trees in the Canal after the flood in Dezhou

第 190-195 页：**走在运河线上（组照）** 周璐
Pages 190-195: **Walking on the Canal line (Series)** Zhou Lu

聊城江北水城
Jiangbei water city in Liaocheng

德州三湾抵一闸
Sanwan converges into one lock in Dezhou

枣庄台儿庄古城
Taierzhuang ancient town in Zaozhuang

德州减河
Jian River in Dezhou

德州董子读书台
Dongzi Reading Platform in Dezhou

济宁火头湾通济闸
Tongji Lock on Huotouwan in Jining

济宁南阳古镇的桥
The bridge in Nanyang ancient town, Jining

水箭，大运河嘉兴段 1980 年代初，嘉兴，周向阳
Shuiduan on the Grand Canal Jiaxing section. Early 1980s, Jiaxing, Zhou Xiangyang

西湖文化广场 杭州，1999 年，刘浩源
West Lake cultural plaza. Hangzhou, 1999, Liu Haoyuan

俯瞰雪域天堂塔 2022 年，洛阳，肖博
Overlooking the snowland Paradise Tower. 2022, Luoyang, Xiao Bo

收茭白的村民　德清，2021 年 4 月
Villagers harvesting water bamboo ．Deqing, April 2021

第 198-203 页：**运河记忆（组照）**　钟黎明
Pages 198-203：**Canal Memories (Series)**．Zhong Liming

村民在运送椽子　绍兴，2019 年 11 月
Villagers transporting roof rafters . Shaoxing, November 2019

船老大的孩子　杭州，2022 年 1 月
Boatman's child ．Hangzhou, January 2022

台风来了，过往船舶进港避风　杭州，2015 年 7 月
Typhoon approaches, ships seek shelter in the harbor ． Hangzhou, July 2015

运河广场上两位年轻人在晨读　杭州，2019 年 8 月
Two young people reading at dawn on the Canal Square ． Hangzhou, August 2019

捻螺蛳的老人　德清，2019 年 12 月
An old man picking river snails ．Deqing, December 2019

通州渡口 2008 年，黑建军
Tongzhou Ferry. 2008, Hei Jianjun

36 年跨度的苏州农村婚礼对比（组照）　韦鸣
A Comparative Study of Rural Weddings in Suzhou Spanning 36 Years (Series). Wei Ming

开船啦，河埠头站满了家人和亲朋好友。
Sailing away! The riverbank is filled with family and friends.

亲人和闺蜜陪伴新娘子到新郎家中。
Relatives and best friends accompany the bride to the groom's Home.

电视机、缝纫机、电冰箱、自行车等嫁妆装了满满两船。
TV, sewing machine, refrigerator, bicycle, and other dowry
Items fill two boats to the brim.

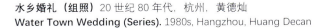

水乡婚礼（组照）20 世纪 80 年代，杭州，黄德灿
Water Town Wedding (Series). 1980s, Hangzhou, Huang Decan

新娘子到新郎家附近，新郎舅舅会把新娘子抱进家门。
When the bride arrives near the groom's home, the groom's uncle will carry the bride into the house.

第 210-213 页：**运河婚典（组照）** 杭州，廖雄
Pages 210-213 : **Canal wedding ceremony (Series).** Hangzhou, Liao Xiong

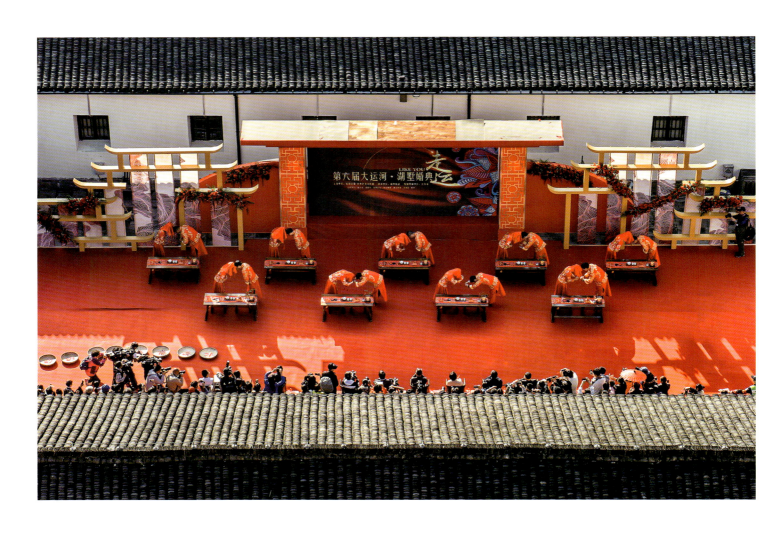

抛绣球招亲
Throwing a ball to find a husband

街头变脸表演
Street face-changing performance

第 214-217 页：运河风情（组照） 贾传军
Pages 214-217：**Canal Scenery (Series).** Jia Chuanjun

丰收的柳条
Harvest of willow branches

芡实地里追肥
Fertilizing the water chestnuts

运河岸边看大船
Watching the big ships on the canal bank

微山湖里的游客
Tourists in Weishan Lake

运河岸边休闲的人们
People relaxing on the canal bank

华灯初上窑湾镇
Lights come on in Yaowan Town

古镇迎瑞雪　杭州，张丽娟
Welcome snow in the ancient town. Hangzhou, Zhang Lijuan

塘栖 杭州，孙新尖
Tangqi, Hangzhou. Hangzhou, Sun Xinjian

在希望的田野上 杭州，金红霞
In the fields of hope. Hangzhou, Jin Hongxia

捕鱼 镇江，孙继生
Fishing. Zhenjiang, Sun Jisheng

博陆搪瓷厂工人 杭州，沈杰
Worker at Bolu Enamel Factory. Hangzhou, Shen Jie

运河码头采藕工 扬州，朱崇平
Lotus root harvester at the canal dock. Yangzhou, Zhu Chongping

河湖卫士 杭州，林天立
Guardian of rivers and lakes. Hangzhou, Lin Tianli

守护大运河 沧州，赫华
Guardian of the Grand Canal. Cangzhou, He Hua

大运河边的酒匠（组照）杭州，李盛韬
The distilled spirit craftsman by the Grand Canal (Series). Hangzhou, Li Shengtao

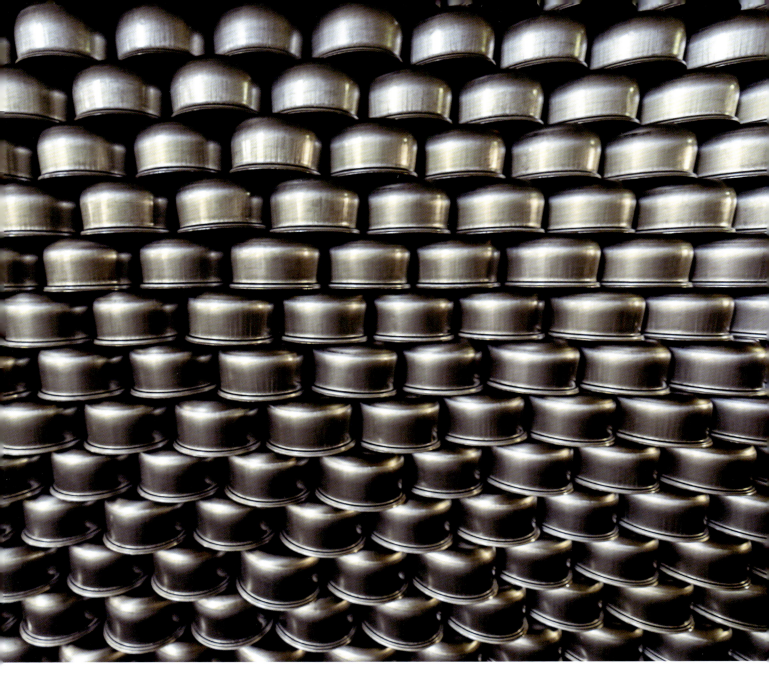

搪瓷厂（组照）杭州，倪伟
Enamel Factory (Series). Hangzhou, Ni Wei

形神兼备六合拳（组照）沧州，刘连升
Six Harmony Fist (Series). Cangzhou, Liu Liansheng

塘栖肖像（组照）杭州，周佳清
Portrait of Tangqi (Series). Hangzhou, Zhou Jiaqing

大运河畔欢乐颂　镇江，韦夕瑾
Joyful ode by the Grand Canal. Zhenjiang, Wei Xijin

蜕变 杭州余杭区仓前街道，黄德灿
Transformation, Cangqian Street, Yuhang District. Hangzhou, Huang Decan

运河上的璀璨明珠——开封鼓楼夜市 李怀正
The brilliant pearl on the Grand Canal - Kaifeng Drum Tower night market, Li Huaizheng

运河上的皮影戏 杭州，应召平
Shadow play on the Grand Canal. Hangzhou, Ying Zhaoping

运河长卷：行走大运河　杭州，应召平
The long scroll of the Grand Canal: walking along the Grand Canal. Hangzhou, Ying Zhaoping

后 记
POSTSCRIPT

追溯大运河影像发展的脉络

    2018 年 11 月，来自大运河南端城市杭州的一批摄影人开始了大运河的拍摄创作之旅。2019 年大运河文化带建设成为国家战略之后，杭州摄影人以更高的热情参与大运河影像文化的创作、挖掘和传播工作。

    最开始是沿着大运河采风创作，用镜头记录大运河的景观和两岸的风土人情，感受大运河博大精深的人文底蕴。到 2022 年 12 月，杭州摄影人完成了隋唐运河、京杭大运河和浙东运河全程的拍摄创作。行走拍摄创作之余，走访大运河沿线摄影家协会，在中国摄影家协会相关领导的支持下，共同发起成立大运河摄影发展联盟，并于 2019 年 9 月在杭州首次举办联盟成员签约仪式。从此，大运河沿线摄影界创作、展览和交流活动不断，联盟成员也不断增多。到 2023 年 12 月，联盟成员发展到了 37 家，大型大运河主题摄影活动每年至少举办一两次。这些活动丰富了大运河沿线的摄影创作和交流。

    浙江的大运河沿线城市杭州、嘉兴、绍兴等地活跃着一批老照片收藏家，他们时常交流雅聚，频繁出席老照片拍卖会，联手购买大宗藏品，组织老照片原作展，出版相关研究书籍，被誉为老照片收藏界的"浙江现象"。近年来，他们把大运河影像的收集作为重点，把目光投向海外境外，使早期的大运河老照片原作源源不断回到国内，填补了大运河影像的空白，也勾画出近 200 年来大运河历史影像的轮廓。在此基础上，杭州市摄影家协会组织人员通过网络或利用出国交流、留学等机会，到国外图书馆、博物馆、档案馆等机构搜寻中国大运河的历史影像，经过几年的努力，积累了大量老照片原作，使大运河影像发展的脉络不断清晰，影像史体系不断完善。

    2023 年 6 月，在杭州临平区举办的"运河中国"首届影像艺术周活动，是对大运河影像文化的一次综合探索和展示。在举办"运河中国"影像大展的同时，杭州市摄影家协会、杭州运河辰和博物院有限公司与中国摄影出版社联合组织了《大运河影像年鉴（2023 年）》（以下简称《年鉴》）的作品征集出版工作，召开"运河的影像叙事"学术研讨会，组织大运河沿线摄影家进行采风创作，旨在从历史演变和学术层面为大运河影像文化做些探索。

    借出版《年鉴》的机会，经编委会确定，由张友国对 1949 年以前的大运河影像简史进行梳理，由扬州大学的杨健副教授整理新中国运河影像简史。《年鉴》还收录了近几年大运河影像文化研究的一些文章，试图从当代视角探讨大运河影像的现代特点，梳理大运河影像发展的脉络，读出大运河影像的文化基因图谱，为大运河影像文化构建引来源头活水。

这次出版的《运河中国》，没有对展览的内容照搬照抄。执行主编沈珂先生的编辑意图显示，他希望通过编辑本画册，对入展摄影作品的艺术性和人文精神进行再凝练再提升，对大运河影像发展历程进行再梳理再概括，对大运河影像文化进行再回顾再致敬。可以看出，沈珂先生编辑本画册是用心的，取得了良好的效果。

值此《运河中国》出版之际，特别感谢中国摄影家协会李舸主席、杨越峦副主席长期以来的关心、指导和参与，使活动增光添彩！

感谢杭州临平区委宣传部、临平区文联、临平区摄协和杭州运河辰和博物院有限公司给予的大力支持。

感谢总策展人崔波老师和他充满朝气的策展团队，为大家奉献上了大运河影像的文化大餐。

感谢本书执行主编沈珂先生，正是在他的不懈努力下，本画册艺术水准得以不断提升。

感谢老照片收藏家韩一飞、徐忠民、杜晓华、楼立伟、张结、江建平、高国忠、纪元、李长江、方林峰等先生，他们以自己收藏的老照片为这次展览增色增辉，为大运河发展历史提供影像实证，为大运河影像体系提供新鲜佐证和丰富补充。

感谢大运河沿线的摄影家、大运河摄影发展联盟的各位同仁提供的大量精品力作，使新时代大运河影像文化呈现新的特色！

是为后记。

张友国
2024 年 12 月于杭州

作者系浙江省摄影家协会副主席、杭州市摄影家协会主席，大运河摄影发展联盟发起人，中国大运河老照片收藏者。

Tracing the Development of Grand Canal Images

In November 2018, a group of photographers from Hangzhou, a city located at the southern end of the Grand Canal, embarked on a journey to capture the essence of the Grand Canal through their lenses. After the Grand Canal Cultural Belt construction became a national strategy in 2019, photographers from Hangzhou became even more enthusiastic about participating in the creation, exploration, and dissemination of Grand Canal imagery culture.

It all began with field trips along the Grand Canal, where everyone used their cameras to document the magnificent landscapes and the local customs on both banks, experiencing the profound cultural heritage of the Grand Canal. By December 2022, they had completed the full journey of photographing the Sui-Tang Grand Canal, the Beijing-Hangzhou Grand Canal, and the Zhejiang East Grand Canal. While engaging in photography, they also visited photography associations along the Grand Canal. With the support of relevant leaders from China Photographers Association, they jointly initiated the establishment of Grand Canal Photography Development Alliance. In September 2019, the alliance held its inaugural member signing ceremony in Hangzhou. Since then, activities and exchanges within the photography community along the Grand Canal have been ongoing,and creative and exhibition exchange activities holding whenever possible. By December 2023, the alliance had grown to include 37 members, and large-scale Grand Canal-themed photography events were held at least once or twice a year. These activities enriched photography creation and exchanges along the Grand Canal.

In Zhejiang Province, cities along the Grand Canal such as Hangzhou, Jiaxing, and Shaoxing are home to a group of antique photograph collectors. They often gather to exchange ideas, frequently attend antique photograph auctions, collectively purchase large collections, organize exhibitions of original antique photographs, and publish related research books. They have been acclaimed as the "Zhejiang Phenomenon" in the antique photograph collecting community. In recent years, they have focused on collecting Grand Canal imagery, directing their attention overseas and bringing back early original Grand Canal photographs to fill the gaps in Grand Canal imagery and outline the historical imagery of the Grand Canal over the past 200 years. Building upon this foundation, Hangzhou Photographers Association has organized personnel to search for historical Grand Canal imagery in overseas libraries, museums, archives, and other institutions through online exchanges, studying abroad, and other opportunities. After several years of effort, they have accumulated a large number of original antique photographs, continuously clarifying the development trajectory of Grand Canal imagery and improving the system of visual history.

"China Stories about the Grand Canal" Image Art Week and Exhibition, held in Linping District, Hangzhou in June 2023, was a comprehensive exploration and exhibition of the image culture of the Grand Canal.Alongside the "China Stories about the Grand Canal" Photography Exhibition, the Hangzhou Photographers Association, Hangzhou Grand Canal Chenhe Museum Co., Ltd., and China Photography Press jointly organized the *Grand Canal Image Yearbook (2023)* work collection and publication, convened the "Image Narrative of the Grand Canal" academic symposium, and organized photographers along the Grand Canal to conduct field trips and creative work. The aim was to explore the image culture of the Grand Canal from historical evolution and academic perspectives.

Taking the opportunity of publishing *Grand Canal Image Yearbook*, it was decided by the editorial board that Zhang Youguo would compile a brief history of Grand Canal imagery before 1949, while Associate Professor Yang Jian from Yangzhou University would compile a brief history of post-1949 Grand Canal imagery. The Yearbook also included some articles from recent years on the study of Grand Canal imagery culture, attempting to explore the modern characteristics of Grand Canal imagery from a contemporary visual perspective, clarify the development trajectory of Grand Canal imagery, and decipher the cultural genealogy of Grand Canal imagery, thereby constructing a source of inspiration for Grand Canal imagery culture.

The publication of "China Stories about the Grand Canal" did not simply replicate the content of the exhibition. The editorial intention of Chief Editor Shen Ke demonstrated his desire to refine and enhance the artistic and humanistic aspects of the exhibited photography works, to retrace and summarize the development process of Grand Canal imagery, and to review and pay tribute to Grand Canal imagery culture. It is evident that Mr. Shen Ke edited this catalog with great care, achieving excellent results.

On the occasion of the publication of the "China Stories about the Grand Canal", special thanks are extended to Chairman Li Ge and Vice Chairman Yang Yueluan of China Photographers Association for their long-term care, guidance, and participation, which added luster to the event!

We would like to express our sincere thanks to the Publicity Department of Linping District Committee, Linping Federation of Literary and Art Circles, Linping Photographers Association, and the Hangzhou Canal Chenhe Museum Co., Ltd. for their strong support.

Thanks to Chief Curator Cui Bo and his energetic curatorial team for presenting a cultural feast of Grand Canal imagery.

We extend our gratitude to Mr. Shen Ke, the executive editor of this book, whose relentless efforts have continuously elevated the artistic standard of this album.

Special thanks to antique photograph collectors Mr. Han Yifei, Mr. Xu Zhongmin, Mr. Du Xiaohua, Mr. Lou Liwei, Mr. Zhang Jie, Mr. Jiang Jianping, Mr. Gao Guozhong, Mr. Ji Yuan, Mr. Li Changjiang, Mr. Fang Linfeng, and others. Their collections of antique photographs added brilliance to this exhibition and provided visual evidence for the historical development of the Grand Canal, as well as fresh evidence and rich supplements to the Grand Canal imagery system.

We are deeply grateful to the photographers along the Grand Canal and the colleagues of the Grand Canal Photography Development Alliance for providing a wealth of exquisite works, showcasing a new character of the Grand Canal's image culture in the new era!

This is the postscript.

Zhang Youguo
Hangzhou, December 2024

The author is the Vice Chairman of Zhejiang Photographers Association, Chairman of Hangzhou Photographers Association, initiator of Grand Canal Photography Development Alliance, and a collector of antique Grand Canal photographs.

出版信息

《"运河中国"首届影像大展作品集》编委会

主　　任　　高　扬　沈　威　张友国
副 主 任　　杭建卫　戚向阳
成　　员　　吴根年　黄德灿　徐　静　高　山
　　　　　　韩一飞　安　苹　倪　伟　张晏子
主　　编　　张友国
执行主编　　沈　珂
编辑校对　　安　苹

支持单位　　临平区大运河（超山）文化研究中心
　　　　　　中共杭州市临平区委宣传部
　　　　　　杭州市临平区文学艺术界联合会

Publication Information

Editorial Board of *"China Stories about the Grand Canal" The First Photographic
Exhibition Works Collection*

Editorial Board
Chairperson: Gao Yang
Vice Chairpersons: Shen Wei, Zhang Youguo
Members: Hang Jianwei, Qi Xiangyang, Wu Gennian, Huang Dechan, Xu Jing, Gao Shan,
Han Yifei, An Ping, Ni Wei, Zhang Yanzi
Editorial Team
Chief Editor: Zhang Youguo
Executive Editor: Shen Ke
Editors & Proofreaders: An Ping

Supported by:
Linping Grand Canal (Chaoshan) Cultural Research Center
The Publicity Department of the CPC Linping District Committee of Hangzhou
Hangzhou Linping District Federation of Literary and Art Circles

图书在版编目（CIP）数据

运河中国 / 张友国编 . -- 北京 : 中国摄影出版传

媒有限责任公司 , 2024. 6. -- ISBN 978-7-5179-1446-4

Ⅰ . K928.42-64

中国国家版本馆 CIP 数据核字第 2025VU3987 号

书　　　名：运河中国

主　　　编："运河中国"影像大展组委会 杭州市摄影家协会

出 品 人：高扬

责任编辑：徐静

装帧设计：沈珂

出　　　版：中国摄影出版传媒有限责任公司（中国摄影出版社）

　　　　　　地址：北京市东城区东四十二条 48 号　　邮编：100007

　　　　　　发行部：010—65136125　　65280977

　　　　　　网址：www.cpph.com

　　　　　　邮箱：distribution@cpph.com

印　　　刷：北京启航东方印刷有限公司

开　　　本：16 开

印　　　张：15.5

版　　　次：2025 年 3 月第 1 版

印　　　次：2025 年 3 月第 1 次印刷

ISBN 978-7-5179-1446-4

定　　　价：320.00 元